HOW
POWER SELLING
BROUGHT ME SUCCESS
IN 6 HOURS

HOW POWER SELLING

BROUGHT ME

Englewood Cliffs, N. J.

PRENTICE-HALL, INC.

SUCCESS

IN **6** HOURS

by DR. PIERCE P. BROOKS

PRINTED IN THE UNITED STATES OF AMERICA

40065

FOREWORD

SOME NINE YEARS AGO, I HAD KNOWN PIERCE P. Brooks as an ordinary salesman. Then I suddenly realized that something had happened to him. Pierce had found the trick of turning an ordinary salesman into a successful salesman and, at the same time, discovered how to win friends and personal happiness by helping others achieve a better way of life.

At the age of 45, when some men begin to think that their opportunities lie behind them, Pierce made a new start. He organized the National Bankers Life Insurance Company, and from a meager beginning he built it into a very successful company. However, his business success is only a part of the story of a successful salesman. For example, a short time after he was elected Chairman of the Board of Stewards of the Tyler Street Methodist Church, Dallas, Texas, that church set an all-time record for Sunday School attendance.

When he was elected President of the Texas Legal Reserve Officials Association, the Association had only 36 members. When he stepped down as President, after his one-year term, the Association had increased its membership to 69 participating companies.

Perhaps it is more than a coincidence that Dallas, Texas, has for a number of years held the record as one of the nation's safest cities, and added to that, Pierce Brooks was the first President of the Texas Safety Council.

I think Pierce Brooks is a top-flight salesman. Regardless of what you sell, this book should be helpful to you and to all who sell.

R. L. THORNTON

What This Book Will Do For You

I WAITED NINE YEARS TO WRITE THIS BOOK. Nine years ago something happened to me that changed my life within six hours' time.

I was out of a job at the time. Today, I am head of my own insurance company, a 10-million dollar firm, and am affiliated with real estate companies, mortgage and loan companies, banking interests, and am at the present time setting up a School of Business Administration at one of our leading colleges. I mention this only by way of contrast between my present position, and what it was nine years ago.

My Discovery of Power Selling

Back there, at the age of 45, I discovered what I call POWER SELLING. It was through salesmanship that I achieved whatever success I have had in the past nine years.

Within a year after my "new start," various people would say, "Pierce, you ought to write a book."

I had no desire to write a book at the time because I could not see where it would serve any useful purpose to tell the world merely what Pierce P. Brooks had done or could do.

But after nine years of *testing*, I have seen that POWER SELLING TECHNIQUES that helped me can help anyone—that my story is not really the story of a man, but a *method*.

This method has proved to be applicable to any field of selling—insurance, automobiles, real estate, savings accounts, specialty, or door-to-door selling, and just about every other field you could imagine. It has also been used in various fields that we ordinarily do not classify as "selling."

Power Selling Used by Hundreds of Salesmen

Hundreds of other people have proved that they could use POWER SELLING as well as I could. In fact, if this method couldn't have been used by others, I would have no story to write about. The success of all the various businesses with which I am associated has been due in large part to the fact that we have had *successful salesmen* working for us. It is these men and women on the firing line who have made these companies grow. No sales executive can be successful unless he has successful salesmen and saleswomen working for and with him.

Many of our salesmen and saleswomen had no previous sales experience before coming with our companies. Yet, they have been outstanding producers, and many of their stories are more sensational than my own.

One evening Governor Allan Shivers of Texas, a personal friend, and I were talking about these successful men and women and how they had found themselves.

Allan said, "Pierce, there are millions of other Americans in this country who are in the same boat you were nine years ago—not failing completely, never succeeding completely—just getting by. The men and women in your own companies have proved that other people can profit by your POWER SELLING. Why don't you go ahead and write that book?"

So I wrote it.

Three Requirements for Success

Whoever you are, however much you may have failed in the past, I can assure you of this:

You can succeed in life—

1. If you learn to *use* the Power that's locked up in you,

2. You learn *where* to apply that Power,

3. You learn *how* to apply that Power.

That is what I hope to be able to show you something about in this book.

P. P. B.

CONTENTS

ix

HOW
POWER SELLING
BROUGHT ME SUCCESS
IN SIX HOURS

SIX HOURS THAT CHANGED MY LIFE

AT 12 O'CLOCK, ONE BLACK NIGHT NINE YEARS ago, I was broke and out of a job.

Six hours later I had $37,000 and was headed for a new start in life. This start was to lead me, at the age of 45, to the presidency of three insurance companies, a directorship in a bank, my own real estate companies, and a number of other successful business ventures.

During the 20 years leading up to that turning point in my life, I had not been a total failure. I suppose that I was an average salesman. I worked hard and long to provide the minimum that a person can get by on and still rear a family.

I lived in a modest $6,000 house (bought back when homes were cheaper). I went to church, but was not active in church work. I belonged to a few clubs, always a member, but never an officer. I ran for public office, received a commendable vote, but was not elected. I attended sales meetings, but was never called on to take an active part. I was not unliked by people, but had only a few friends I could count on. I went to social functions, but was never "recognized."

I was "comfortable," in a cramped, half-frustrated sort of way—but yet I was not a total failure; I was just a luke-warm success. And I sometimes think that a luke-warm success is worse than failure. For I endured luke-warm success for 20 years without doing anything about it. It was only when I saw total failure staring me in the face that I was able to get out of my rut.

The danger of "doing the best I can." If you learn to rationalize, you can kid yourself into believing that you are

"doing the best you can," as long as you are a luke-warm success. You convince yourself that you really couldn't do any
better than you're doing.

I *wanted* to be successful during those 20 years. I even
"tried" to be. I worked hard. But somehow I didn't make the
grade. I made payments on one automobile and a home, and
that was all.

I read every success story I could get my hands on, hoping
to find the secret, but somehow it eluded me. I studied sales
psychology and sales techniques. But somehow they wouldn't
seem to work for me. Something seemed to be missing.

The spur of my business collapse. I might have continued
coasting along, kidding myself that I was doing all I could,
except for one thing: I lost my job. I had had my eye on an
insurance agency contract and thought I had it "made." But
my contract, my only source of income, was cancelled over-
night. The insurance company would no longer accept my applications for insurance. At eight o'clock the next morning
my agents would be forced to associate with other firms. My
last hopes of a successful general agency would go with them.
I had just 24 hours between me and failure—spelled with a
capital "F."

For years I had dreamed of going into business for myself.
Naturally, during my "black hours," I thought of forming a
company and starting over. But that would take months—
months of talking with prospective investors to raise the necessary thousands. It would be hard. But my time was limited.
I had to do something within just 24 hours—or tell my salesmen I had no more work for them. They would be gone beyond
recall. I could not finance my personal expenses over a long
period of time.

My First Act in Defeating Failure

I tried to hedge. I tried to find a way out, some compromise
solution. But this time, circumstances had backed me into a
corner. There were no easy ways out. I was 45 years old and
it might be my last chance. And I didn't have forever to
think about it.

"Pierce, old boy," I said to myself, "The time has come for you to change your way of thinking and your way of doing. You can go on as you have been for 20 years and within 24 hours you'll be a failure."

The first thing I did was to *make a definite decision to organize my own business.*

At the time I didn't know how I was to organize it. I just knew that I was going to do it—or bust! As soon as I made this definite decision, I felt better although my outward position had not changed in the slightest. I stopped feeling sorry for myself. I stopped being scared. I stopped worrying about all the things that *might* happen, and was able to concentrate all my mental and spiritual powers upon just one thing: "How am I going to do it?"

In short, I was able to let go my negative thoughts and adopt a positive attitude about the situation.

Securing capital through salesmanship. How would I organize a business? The most obvious answer, of course, was that I would have to raise capital. So I sat down and made up a list of 35 businessmen whom I had met during the past 20 years and knew well. (Strange that I had never even taken this first step before.)

"How can I convince these men to invest their money in me?" I asked myself.

"By using salesmanship," was the obvious answer.

Although I had been selling for 20 years, I next asked myself,

"Just what is salesmanship, anyway, and how can I best use it in this situation?"

For the next several hours I sat at my desk and wrote down every single thing that I could think of that was important in making a sale. I drew on my knowledge of 20 years and tried to distill it into its basic essentials.

I soon found out something about myself. Although I would have denied it the week before, I now saw that actually I had not been *using* more than 25 per cent of what I knew. At least 75 per cent of my sales power was lying idle. I had listened to dozens of sales talks and had read scores of books on such basic things as "gaining attention," "creating desire" . . . and

I had supposed that I had been using them. If I ever gave any thought to their actual application to my job, it was in a vague sort of way. "Sure, I'll try to remember to gain attention."

How I applied the magic of salesmanship to my own problem. But now that it really mattered, I got down to cases. How could these various elements of the sale be applied specifically to this situation?

I worked out a sales pitch embodying all the power factors of salesmanship I could think of. Then I tailored this sales talk somewhat to fit each individual prospect. For example, one of my prospects was a prominent surgeon.

When he objected that he needed more time to think it over, I said, "Doc, you, of all people, should know that sometimes very important consequences can depend upon making a decision within a very short time. This is what you might call an 'emergency operation.' "

When he hesitated, I said, "Doc, I am going to organize a company and make a lot of money for a small, preferred group. But I can't wait. I start the wheels turning tomorrow morning. If you are going to 'operate,' you are going to have to do it now. Otherwise, this 'patient' of mine here named 'opportunity' is going to be dead, as far as you are concerned."

That day, while trying to analyze and classify my 20 years' experience of salesmanship into some readily available plan that could be used, I hit upon the rudiments of a formula that I call POWER SELLING. I didn't have the formula worked out then—I had only its beginning—but I knew I had something.

How I Used My Selling Techniques to Raise $37,000

The next thing I did back there that day was to *get into action.*

The old saying, "Knowledge is power," is only partly true. For 20 years I had stored up all sorts of knowledge about selling. But I certainly was far from powerful. It would be more correct to say that "Knowledge is potential power." It is said that all of us "know better than we do," and I have found that was certainly true in my own case.

Knowledge becomes power only at the point that it is put into action. That is why, although I spent 24 hours—or 20 years (depending on how you look at it) leading up to those important six hours, I say that I "found" success in those six hours. For it was only in those six hours that I got any results.

By the time I had made up my mind to do something about my situation, and had worked out my plan of what I was going to do and how I was going to do it, it was midnight.

Well, I certainly had a good excuse for postponing action. After all, it was 12 o'clock at night. But there was one thing wrong with this excuse. My deadline was at 8 the next morning if I was going to hold my salesmen. I had already made the decision to do something about the situation.

Using two of salesmanship's most important elements. After all, why not call up my prospects at midnight? Two of the essentials of salesmanship I had worked out were "be spectacular," and "hold attention." Well, what would be more spectacular than getting a man up out of bed in the middle of the night for a long-distance phone call? What better opportunity to hold his attention—when he would have absolutely nothing else on his mind? In fact, he would be "all ears" to find out why in the world Pierce P. Brooks was calling this time of night.

There was one other thing. I had worked out a plan for a business enterprise that I was sure would make all my investors some money. I felt sure I could convince them of this. Why apologize for getting a man up out of bed to tell him you were going to make him some money? I had already firmly convinced myself that this was the case.

The Phone Conversation That Started Me Toward $1,000,000

So I picked up the telephone and placed my first call. In a few minutes I heard the operator say, "Go ahead, sir." It was the best advice I ever had.

I was a little hesitant when I heard the click at the other end of the line, and I almost cancelled the call. But when the long-distance operator said, "Go ahead, sir," I went ahead!

"Is that you, Doc?"

Dr. Carl J. Wieland, a physician in Austin, Texas, sounded sleepy.

"Hello, Pierce. What's the matter? What's on your mind at this time of night?"

"Doc, I'm forming a new life insurance company. It's going to be the greatest insurance company Texas ever had. I thought you'd like a chance to get in on it, so I've set aside an interest for you."

"Well . . . uh . . . fine. Drop in to see me when you're out this way and we'll talk it over."

"Doc, I can make money for both of us if I can raise $37,000 in the next six hours. Remember, there have been millions made out of Insurance Stocks — funds invested in the Bankers Reserve Insurance Company Stock have earned for the founders over $4,000 for each $100 invested — there's more I could say, but I don't have time to explain. How much can I put you down for?"

This was too much for Doctor Wieland, and too fast.

"Now wait a minute," he said, "I can't buy into an insurance company without looking it over first. What's the matter, Pierce? Do you think I'm crazy? What kind of a businessman do you think I am?"

"If I didn't think you were a shrewd businessman, I wouldn't be calling you. I felt you would want to get in on the ground floor with a few personal friends. There's no time to think it over. I'm offering you a chance of a lifetime. I'm not asking you for a favor; I'm offering you an opportunity. But you'll have to decide now. The wheels start rolling in the morning, and this is going to be a company like you never saw before."

"Pierce, I just can't decide on such short notice."

"You don't have to decide anything. Just send me a check in a couple of days, when you've thought it over. All I need now is your nod. I am setting aside $1,500 of stock for you, which is the maximum I am offering any one of my friends in the Preferred Group."

"I am a fool to say yes, but put me down for $1,500," he said.

As I hung up the receiver, my hesitation vanished. If I could sell Dr. Wieland, I could sell others.

In the next few hours I called people all over the Southwest. They were sleepy, confused, indignant, and exasperated. I didn't convince them all, but 24 were sold on the idea, and at four o'clock in the morning I drained the last cup of coffee from the pot and lay back exhausted. I had $37,000 pledged to organize an Insurance Company that was destined to skyrocket into a $10,000,000 company within eight years.

My mind ran back to the evening before and the events that led up to the more than 30 hurried night-time calls. It was difficult to realize that just six hours before I had been facing what had looked like failure.

Six hours later, when I hung up the phone, I had $37,000. But I had something more. I had found a new way of life. I had learned some of the most important lessons in my life.

You build success; you can't create it. Now, I want to make it clear why I say I found success within those six hours. I didn't suddenly come up with a plan for a business within those six hours. For 20 years I had been working on that. I had planned it out. I had made notes. I had ideas written down on just how I would run my own real estate business, my mortgage business, and maybe my own insurance business — "someday."

I had a definite plan worked out for how I would run my real estate business. Many times I had said to myself, "If I ever had an insurance business of my own, I would run it such-and-such a way."

I had a sound plan worked out. But this plan had no *power*. It was gathering dust. It had never made me successful, and after 20 years my reward was failure.

For 20 years I had studied salesmanship — and I knew a lot about salesmanship. Yet salesmanship had never made me anything other than a luke-warm success, sometimes up, sometimes down.

It was only during those six hours that my knowledge of salesmanship, and my planning and dreaming to own my own business, ever amounted to anything.

It was during those six hours that I *found* success.

It was during those six hours that I discovered POWER SELLING.

I didn't discover all there is to know about POWER SELLING in those six hours, and I haven't discovered all there is to know about it in the past nine years. We say that "Columbus discovered America," when he only landed on an island off the coast. We realize that Columbus did not know *all* about the continent of North America at the time of his discovery. We realize that he could not have drawn an accurate map of the country he is credited with discovering.

So, when I say I "discovered" power selling, all I mean to convey is that I landed on a shore that was new to me. I had discovered something that to me, at least — was a new world of selling. I didn't know too much about it at the time, but I knew I had made an important discovery. It started me off on an adventure that is still going on.

Also, when I say I found success, I do not mean that I found a destination, but rather a road. *Success* is a relative term. In terms of what I had been before, perhaps I was a success six hours later. But I do not like to think of myself as having arrived at success. For it is my experience that once a man decides that he has "arrived," he loses all "git-up-and-git." He doesn't need it, for there's nowhere to go.

I did get my feet on the "success road"; whereas I had been travelling a failure road.

I started on a journey back there nine years ago. It's the journey, and the things I've learned along the way, that I want to tell you about in this book.

I want to tell you how I discovered the seven keys for unlocking your sales power; how I discovered the "five-course-dinner" method of sales techniques that has built five successful businesses; how one simple technique enabled an associate of mine to make a $500,000 sale; and how another friend of mine, with whom I am associated in another business, used a simple technique for closing, and made a million-dollar sale.

Now let me tell you about the way that I discovered a method for unfastening the gates to an unlimited source of power — power that quickly lifted me to the road toward business success.

1

HOW I DISCOVERED A KEY
FOR UNLOCKING SALES POWER

ALTHOUGH I DIDN'T REALIZE JUST WHAT HAD happened to me at the time, I was fortunate enough, when I was faced with a crisis, to stumble onto an age-old secret of releasing inner power, and I made the decision to go forward.

All I knew at the time was that within a matter of hours I had somehow tapped a source of Power that I had never had before. It was a problem-solving power that enabled my mind to think clearer and faster and to find the solution to my problem by being able to see salesmanship in a new light. I had more energy, more self-confidence. My thoughts, which had been so negative, seemed to become more and more positive. Old timidities and fears seemed to fall away.

As soon as I "settled down" from the excitement of having raised the $37,000, however, I determined that I would find the answer. For a matter of a few hours I had been able to "sell over my head." During those six hours, as prospect after prospect bought, I got the feeling that anything was possible. No venture was too great for me to tackle.

Then, gradually, I began to sink back into old habits of thinking and doing. I began to wonder whether I hadn't laid out too ambitious a plan for myself.

It was at this time that Charles Dunne, President, Dunne's Insurance Reports, placed in my hands a copy of a little book by an English psychologist, J. A. Hadfield, called *The Psychology of Power.**

The Power That Springs from Necessity

Well, I read the little book and discovered that my own experience was not at all unique. It was common experience for men and women in times of emergency suddenly to find themselves with new powers, mental, physical, and spiritual.

We have all heard stories of people performing superhuman feats of strength in times of dire emergency. We have all heard of invalids who walked or ran from burning buildings, of moral weaklings who became pillars of strength in a pinch. History is full of examples of men and women who have found the answers to pressing problems when they were in a last-ditch situation.

"How wonderful is the way in which, with quite ordinary folk, power leaps to our aid in any time of emergency," wrote Hadfield. "We lead timid lives, shrinking from difficult tasks till perhaps we are forced into them or ourselves determine on them, and immediately we seem to unlock the unseen forces. When we have to face danger, then courage comes; when trial puts a long-continued strain upon us, we find ourselves possessed by the power to endure; or when disaster ultimately brings the fall which we so long dreaded, we feel underneath us the strength as of everlasting arms. *Common experience teaches that, when great demands are made upon us, if only we fearlessly accept the challenge and confidently expend our strength, every danger or difficulty brings its own strength.*"

What I wanted to know was this: how could this power, so evident in time of emergency, be harnessed and put to work in everyday affairs?

Mr. J. H. Perry, Executive Vice President of Union Bankers Insurance Company, was a big help to me in finding the answers and in applying them to our own salesmen.

"Chief," he said to me one day, "I do not believe that emergency or crisis creates any new powers in an individual.

---

* J. A. Hadfield, *The Psychology of Power*. New York: St. Martin's Press.

I think all it does is to *release* powers that are already there. If we could find the key to unlocking these bottled up powers that are already there, but unused, think what it would mean to salesmen."

This started me to thinking along a new line. Suppose that the powers so evident in times of emergency *were* already there, waiting to be used. Why would a crisis release them? If I could find the answer to this, perhaps it would show the way to using other keys to unlocking this power.

Why Crisis Unlocks Power

The best answer I have been able to come up with — and it has proved itself in practice among our salesmen — is this:

The reason we do not customarily use *all our power* is that in ordinary times we divide it up; we even set it to working against itself. We try to use it in too many directions at once. We spend it little by little on a dozen different goals, some of them in conflict with others.

Jesus Christ, the greatest psychologist of all times, told us to keep our eye "single." Most of us, however, do not follow this advice.

Let us take a look at the average salesman, as he starts out in the morning. One of his goals is to sell goods. But, perhaps, without realizing it, he also has a number of other goals. One of them is not to work too hard. He wants to get by with a minimum of effort.

Another goal is that he does not want to appear ridiculous. If he got out and tried to sell for all he was worth — and didn't succeed, he would be admitting to the world and to himself that he was a failure. So, one of his goals is to avoid failure.

Perhaps another goal is to impress prospects with his personal importance. Perhaps, another goal is to enhance his own ego, and not let a prospect get by with insulting him.

He wants to get off early and play golf. He wants to shoot the breeze with the boys. And perhaps a dozen other "wants" or goals are channelling off power that could be used in selling. Fears of various kinds keep our powers bottled up.

Crisis Narrows Our Choice

Open a shot-gun shell, empty it, and place the powder on a table. There is an angle of 180 degrees that it can expend itself in. It literally exerts its force in every direction. If you strike a match to it, it will burn harmlessly. Watching it go up in smoke, it is difficult to realize that this same powder already has great potential power.

Yet, if you take that same amount of powder, confined in a shell, and place the shell in a gun, so that it can expend its force in only one direction — you have a very powerful substance.

Crisis does for us pretty much what you do to the gun powder when you place the shell in the gun. Crisis narrows down our goals to one or two. Where ordinarily we think we have many choices, a crisis brings us face to face with just one choice: Either *DO* — or *DIE*.

Crisis itself has no power. It merely forces us to go *all out* — in one direction, and use all our power on one goal. When we do this, however, it seems indeed, as if new powers have been given us.

How I Made My First Public Speech

I remember when I made my first public speech. I was running for office, but somehow I couldn't bring myself to get up and make a speech. I just "couldn't do it." When I confided my troubles to George Lee, Sales Director, now with Commercial Travelers of Dallas, he advised me to start off gradually, to go out and "practice" my speech in small towns before attempting it in Dallas.

I followed his advice to a degree. I didn't make speeches in surrounding towns, but I did hire a sound truck and would ride up and down streets, reciting a two-minute "spot announcement." Since the sound truck kept moving all the time, I could repeat my two-minute "speech" endlessly.

Then one day I got trapped. We were in Jacksonville, Texas, where there was a farm festival going on, and as we drove slowly by, the crowd closed in around the sound truck. Somebody in the crowd yelled, "Hey, fellows, here is a politician. Let's have a speech." Echoes from the crowd came back, "Yes, if you're running for office, get out and make us a speech."

For a moment I knew panic. If there had been one — just one way — of getting out of there, I would have taken it. But by this time the truck was surrounded by some 2,000 people. There was no way I could retire gracefully. The only way out was to go forward — to go ahead and make a speech.

I don't even remember what I said, but I know that I talked for about 45 minutes off the cuff and that as the speech progressed, the cat calls turned to yells of approval. It probably wasn't a very good speech. But it was tremendously valuable to me — for by being forced into it by crisis, I learned that I *could* speak in public.

Since that time I have spoken thousands of times to all sorts of audiences, and public speaking has played no small part in my business success.

Twenty-Three Sales in Twenty-Four Hours!

I have heard Mr. I. D. Jones, now our South Texas Regional Director, tell how the power of crisis enabled him to make 23 sales in 24 hours. He did this a few months after he came with our company, and when he wasn't too sure himself that he was "cut out to be a salesman."

One day, however, he had seven leads in a town 70 miles away. When he was about half-way there, he suddenly remembered to his horror that he had only 46 cents in his pocket, and that one of the tires on his old car was liable to blow out at any minute.

"I said that if God would get me down there, someone would buy some insurance from me and I would be able to get me a meal and room for that night."

Well, he got there and *immediately began selling*. "I don't believe I knew the word 'no' existed," he said, "I thought it meant 'yes.' "

On his first call, he found his prospect out and immediately began to sell the maid. Just as he was writing the maid up, the ice man came in and without hesitation, he began pitching the ice man.

The ice man appeared interested but complained his ice was melting. Jones asked when he could meet him, and was told, "You can't. I work from 4 o'clock in the morning until late at night."

"Where do you start out from?" asked Jones.

The ice man told him the name of a local filling station. At 4 the next morning, Jones was waiting at the filling station when the ice man showed up. He sold the ice man, ate breakfast, and began calling on businessmen and merchants as they were opening their stores. In one laundry he wrote four applications.

Exactly 24 hours after he began selling, Mr. Jones had written up 23.

How You Can Use the Power of Crisis

"Well," you may say, "I can see where crisis can unlock power. But what good does that do me in everyday life? I don't want to deliberately keep myself on the spot, all the time."

I wondered about this too, and I couldn't see how the power of crisis could be applied every day, until one day Frank Pace, Former Secretary of the Army, gave me an idea that made this power of crisis instantly available.

"The trouble is, Pierce," he said, "most of us are unable to see that *every day is critical*. We kid ourselves that we are not involved in a crisis, just because everything is quiet and we seem to be getting by all right at the moment. But the truth is that we are continually 'on the spot' if we could but see it. What we do or don't do in the present moment is going to be terribly important to our future happiness and fortune. The most precious thing any of us have in the way of an asset is time. Each minute is an opportunity. But when it is gone — it is gone forever."

Well, that too, started me thinking in a new direction.

You are "on the spot." We salesmen are daily *faced with a crisis situation* and all too often do not recognize it as such. The crisis we face is this. Time is the salesman's working capital. Each eight-hour working day the salesman is handed 480 minutes of time. Just because the bank is not about to foreclose on the mortgage and we have a week's supply of groceries in the house or even a large amount of money in the bank, we kid ourselves that *today* is not a critical day.

But let's look at it this way: What you do, or don't do with those 480 critical minutes will determine whether you have *more money* or *less money* in the bank at the end of the month. Salesmen do not get paid for "putting in" a certain number of hours, but for "putting out" during a certain number of hours. A salaried office worker can waste time and it does not immediately affect his pay check. But the salesman gets paid only on *productive time*.

Many salesmen labor under the false impression that they can coast along, waste time, and pull off a big sale that will "make up" for the time wasted. But nothing can ever make up an opportunity wasted. Moreover, it is only by regular, consistent, applied effort, day in and day out that "big sales" are closed.

Every salesman has his "average." One salesman may average $10 in commissions for every productive hour of effort. Another may average $50 in commissions for every productive hour. But, whatever the total commission, statistical studies have shown that over the long pull, it corresponds to the productive hours put in.

Salesmen are paid hourly rates. What this amounts to is this: From a short-sighted view the salesman may appear to be paid "by the job" or only for each successful sale closed. But over a long period, statistics show that the salesman has his own "hourly rate" and that, for all practical purposes, he is paid by the hour. If the salesman could see that all the time he doesn't use productively is stealing money out of his pocket, he can understand that each day is a crisis situation.

This situation requires salesmanship. If you are a sales-manager, you can increase the power of your salesmen to an amazing degree by selling them on the idea that each day is a crisis and that time itself is critical to a salesman. If you are a salesman, sell the idea to yourself.

Are you robbing yourself? I try to bring this home to our

salesmen in many ways. Sometimes, I hold up a thousand dollar bill and announce that this bill really belongs to one of our salesmen, but that he was robbed of it. I then quote production records to show that this man could have earned the thousand dollar bill by working only two additional hours a day for six weeks.

Frank Crowell, Sales Director in Alabama likes to hear me tell this one: Once, one of our salesmen called in and said he would be an hour late to an important sales meeting. He explained his wife was sick and he had to go to the store and get a roll of toilet paper. I figured up the man's average hourly earning, which, as I recall, was about $10.

I then sent out and bought $10 worth of toilet paper and had it unrolled all over the room and piled up all over the table when he came in. When he asked what the gag was, he was advised that this was the amount of toilet paper he cheated himself out of, by going to the store for that one roll; that it would have been cheaper to have had his paper delivered by a taxi, if there was no other way.

This man's sales increased 25 per cent in the next 30 days. Later, he told me, "Dr. Brooks, I was a little chagrined that morning — but you really brought it home to me how much my time was worth. I want to thank you, for it was like putting money in my pocket."

In hot water without knowing it. That is the job you must do for your salesmen, or for yourself, if you would use the Power of Crisis. You must use the same technique on yourself that you would use to sell a prospect. Often, a prospect does not know he has a need until the salesman makes him aware of it. The salesman himself is daily in a crisis, and does not know it unless he brings it home to himself.

If the salesman were advised that every hour during the day he didn't spend selling, someone would *remove* $10, or $15, or $25 from his bank account, he would immediately see the crisis. Yet, that is essentially what he is doing to himself when he fails to make the most of the moment.

Edward Lange, Vice President and Agency Director, gets this point across by telling the story of the frog who was boiled to death *slowly,* by placing him in a pan of cold water, and turning up the flame under the pan very, very slowly. The frog was lazy and had a natural aversion to jumping. After all, he could stand just a small amount of hot water — then just a little more. Finally, however the frog realized too late when he found himself being boiled to death that he had been in a crisis situation and didn't know it.

"Had scalding water been poured in the pan in the beginning," says Mr. Lange, "that frog would have jumped and jumped high. Probably higher than he had ever jumped before. But because that hot water was added gradually, the frog never realized until too late that he was in hot water.

If you're in hot water, jump! "Salesmen," says Mr. Lange, "are all too often like the frog. They go along with the idea that they can 'get by' today and make up for it tomorrow. They go along just 'getting by,' never seeming to realize the big rewards they are missing in life just because they won't put forth the effort to get them. They are in 'hot water' all the time but never realize it, and so they never jump."

You have often heard it said that "depressions make good salesmen." There is no mystery about this. A hungry salesman *knows* he is in a crisis and consequently he is able to use the tremendous power that crisis unlocks. But we do not have to have a depression in order to sell. All we have to do is maintain the same mental attitudes and emotional attitudes — get the same spirit to sell that we have in so-called hard times.

Perhaps this was what Jesus meant when he said, "Blessed are the poor in spirit." If we are "poor in spirit," we do not need an actual depression to wake us up and unlock our powers. If we are "poor," we have wants, and we realize those wants — and the fact that we can realize them — unlocks a power within us to go out after what we want. During the lush war years, a lot of salesmen were "rich in spirit." They had it easy, they didn't want anything any more than they had, and they forgot how to sell.

For 20 years, I was like the frog in Mr. Lange's story. Every day of those 20 years was a day of crisis for me, but I couldn't see it. I was a lukewarm success and a lukewarm failure.

Finally, when the water really got hot, I found I had the power to jump over former obstacles and barriers that had seemed insurmountable.

But I have found since that I do not have to be in desperate financial straits in order to utilize this power. All I have to do to get back into the same "spirit" I had then is this: to sell myself the realization of the crisis that I am facing at the present moment.

POINTS TO REMEMBER

1. In times of crisis everyone has available superhuman power.

2. The mere crisis situation in itself, however, has no power unless you recognize it as a crisis. One man in a burning building may take out a piano singlehandedly. But if he doesn't know the building is on fire he will have no more strength than usual.

3. Everyday, we face many crisis situations that we do not recognize. The present moment is a crisis. What you do with it determines your future. Salesmen are paid "by the hour." Every hour wasted is money out of your pocket.

4. Depressions make good salesmen because a hungry salesman is able to recognize he is in a crisis.

5. However, you do not need to wait for a depression to draw upon your crisis power. All you need to do is keep your hunger alive. Stay hungry for more sales, hungry for a better way of life, hungry for more material comforts.

2

I DISCOVERED THE POWER
OF DECISION

AT THE TIME IT WAS HAPPENING, I DIDN'T HAVE time to figure out why I found myself with new sales power. All I knew was that I had stumbled onto it. But before it would be of any use to me or anyone else, I knew I had to understand it — and be able to "make it happen again."

One day Gus Bowman, Dallas Bank Executive, and I were discussing our mutual friend, Ben Wooten, President of the First National Bank of Dallas. Wooten has had an absolutely phenomenal business success in Texas and Arkansas. One of the secrets of his success in business and everything else, Gus said to me, is that Ben is a "man of decision." When he makes up his mind to do a thing, he does it. When he once makes a decision, it is not a half-way decision, but a 100 per cent decision, unless some new facts enter into the picture.

I went and looked up the word *decision* in my dictionary and found that it came from the Latin word *cisio* meaning *to cut*, and the prefix *de* meaning *from*. Just as the word *incision* means a *cutting into*, the word *decision*, literally means a *cutting off from*. It was once used in that sense.

Miss Mildred Gregory, secretary and treasurer of several companies, had this to say recently: "the real power in decision is the same power that is released in crisis. Decision is just another key to the same power. Both crisis and decision organize us so that we use *all our power* for one goal. Crisis forces us to use our powers on a single objective. Decision enables us to do this for ourselves."

In fact crisis itself has no power and can even ruin you unless you make a decision to go forward in the crisis. All that crisis really does is make it easier for you to make a decision. When faced with only "do — or die," most of us find it easy to make up our minds once and for all to "do."

You sink or swim, depending on your attitude. James F. Lincoln, President of The Lincoln Electric Company, world's largest producer of welding equipment, says:

"Any child *can* swim if thrown into water *if his attempt is to swim.* Many children will drown. The difference between those who swim and those who drown is not difference of latent ability to swim. *It is the lack of attempt* on the part of those who fail. The failures do not try to swim; they are thinking of something else. They are frightened by the new problem and do not try to solve it. They are too busy yelling for help or crying because help is not at hand. Those who try to swim, do swim. They develop from a latent to a real ability."

When you make a 100 per cent decision to do a certain thing, you automatically rule out, or cut yourself off from all courses of action that conflict with your goal.

W. E. Darby, President of National Old Line Insurance Company of Arkansas, had this to say on the subject. "Pierce, the trouble is most of us never completely 'make up our minds.' Our mental powers are not organized or 'made up' toward a certain end. Our decisions are full of 'ifs' and 'maybe's.' Most of us, when we make a decision — even a simple one — keep playing with the idea of some other course. Maybe we didn't decide right. Maybe this decision won't work out. We leave ourselves a 'way out' of a decision, by never giving our 100 per cent mental agreement to the decision."

Make your decision, then relax. William James, writing on this matter of personal power, said, "When once a decision is reached and execution is the order of the day, dismiss ab-

solutely all responsibility and care about the outcome. Un-
clamp, in a word, your intellectual and practical machinery,
and let it run free; and the service it will do you will be twice
as good."

Are You Guilty of Failing?

Esquire magazine reported that when someone asked Ben
Hogan what one big mistake most mediocre golfers made, he
said, "Most of them never completely make up their minds —
even to hit the ball."

One of the secrets of Hogan's own power is certainly the
fact that he could always make up his mind. From the first
tee, he meant to win. After his crippling wreck, a reporter
asked him, when he entered a big tournament, "Do you expect
to win?"

"If I didn't," said Hogan, "I wouldn't be here."

Many salesmen, unfortunately, never make up their minds
that they are going to sell. Their attitude is that "maybe"
they will, or "they would like to," or "I sure hope I can," or
even, "I'm going to try to use my will power." But the POWER
SELLING attitude is, "I am going to do it" — without
reservations.

When I made up my mind to sell nine years ago, it was the
first time in 20 years that I had *completely* made up my mind
to sell. And I sold.

The value of burning your bridges. William the Conqueror
was the only man who ever successfully invaded England.
How did he do it? He burned his boats on the beaches. He
made a 100 per cent decision. He deliberately cut off the only
avenue of escape. There was only one direction to go — only
one way out; he *had* to win. There was no need in worrying
about whether he could get back to the boats or not — there
were no boats there.

It will help you to organize your powers and get them all
channeled in one direction if you will burn your own boats
and your bridges behind you when you make a decision.

The power of a strong decision on your personal life. Several
years ago I decided to quit smoking. I had tried many times

before and had failed. But I decided to try out the power of 100 per cent decision. Before, when I had tried to quit, I had kept toying with the idea of smoking, all the time I had been trying to "not smoke." All the time I was struggling so hard to "not smoke," smoking remained in my own mind as an alternative. Smoking was still a possibility that I considered many times a day.

When I finally quit, however, I listed down all the reasons I could think of why *I wanted* to smoke. Then I listed down all the reasons why I wanted to quit. Since my reasons for quitting far outweighed my reasons for smoking, it seemed only common sense to decide wholeheartedly, once and for all, to quit. By this process, I literally "made up my mind" to quit. No will power was necessary.

Will power implies one part of the personality exerting a *power* or force over the other conflicting parts of the personality. *Will power* is a concept of mental dictatorship in which the "will" forces other parts of the personality into line by sheer strength. This is the method I used when I failed.

When I finally succeeded, I used the democratic method. I took a vote, so to speak, of all the various parts of my personality, and *quit-smoking* won the election. I gave my complete assent to the verdict, and was able to use all the power I had to quit, instead of a part of my power to try to quit and another part not to quit.

When I made this decision, I mentally burned my bridges behind me. I did not consider smoking as a possible alternative; there was no toying with the notion of "how good it would be to smoke."

I realized, however, that the battle was not over; that there would be temptations to change my mind.

How friendship helps your will to power. So I further burned my bridges behind me by announcing to all my friends that I had quit smoking. Then, I could no longer give in to the urge to smoke without losing face. The humiliation of having my friends kid me far outweighed any temptation to smoke. I thus arranged things so that I would actually want to quit smoking more than I would want to smoke.

How You Can Use the Power of Decision

All the outstanding salesmen I know, without exception, make a definite decision either to:

1. Make a certain number of calls per day
2. Put in a certain number of productive hours each day
3. Close a certain number of sales each week.

Sit down in a calm moment and decide for yourself just how many calls you would like to make each hour, or how many hours you need to work, or how many sales you need to close in order to reach some objective. Work out a realistic program that you *can* do. Then decide, once and for all, that you are going to follow this program.

Once you have made this decision, burn your boats behind you. Go on record with your resolve. Tell your plan to your sales manager. Tell all your fellow salesmen. Set yourself a quota of a minimum number of sales you are going to close each week. Do not be unrealistic. The important thing is to make a decision and follow through on it.

Go all out every day. Make up your mind to sell. Remember Ben Hogan's remark about the golfer who can't make up his mind even to hit the ball. Make a decision to sell. Have a little heart-to-heart talk with yourself. Decide that if you are going to sell at all, you are going to go "all out." Remind yourself that when you don't go all out in selling, it is because you really have not fully made up your mind to sell. Go all out on every prospect, big or little. Get the habit of half-way selling on small prospects and soon it becomes a habit.

I sometimes tell my men, "If you're going to sell at all — sell! If you're not going to sell, stay home in bed; but make up your mind one way or the other."

If you can't make up your own mind that you are going to sell the prospect, you'll never succeed in helping him make up his mind that he is going to buy.

From G.I. Joe to insurance executive. Joe F. Luker is today nationally recognized as one of the most successful insurance executives in the country. When he was discharged from the

Army after World War II, he went back to his old field of selling insurance where he had served as an "ordinary salesman" from 1936 to 1942.

He continued as just an "ordinary salesman" until 1948, when, he says, "The thought ran through my mind, 'Why shouldn't I be as capable of running a general insurance agency as anyone else since I had the experience and practically the same background that the agent had that I was working for.' "

One day in 1948 I found myself sitting across the desk from a determined young man of 33. He was telling me he wanted to represent my company as general agent. Moreover, he knew just what he wanted. He wanted an exclusive territory of 64 counties in Southwest Texas. He had very little capital and no experience whatsoever in running a general agency. He had had no experience in recruiting salesmen. He had no organization. To cap it all off, I was not giving out any exclusive agency contracts, at the time, and had no intention of doing so.

Yet, I did give this young man *exactly what he wanted*, and I have never been sorry. The first month his income was over $700. In 1949 he was earning better than $1,200 per month, and today he has a premium income that amounts to approximately $800,000 per year!

I have often asked Joe how he sold me, and always his answer is the same, "I just *made up my mind* I was going to do it."

Apparently, on those rare occasions when a salesman really makes up his mind to sell, the prospect is more or less helpless.

Decide on some long-range goal. Have you "decided" where you want to be ten years from now? You can. And once you have made that decision, it will release a flood of power that will help you in the present. For one thing, it will give you a new power to say "no" to things that would otherwise be a temptation if viewed on a short range basis.

Charles Dunne, President of Dunne's Insurance Reports, Louisville, Ky., and I were talking one day. He said, "Pierce, I like to find out from the man I am interviewing, whether or not he has any long range plans. The man who has no objective other than to live from day-to-day and on a hand-to-mouth basis, has too many temptations." He explains that if a man has a long-range objective, and has made a definite decision to reach it, it becomes easy to say "no" to little day-to-day temptations to loaf, or go to a ball game, or simply shoot the breeze with the boys.

As C. A. Stoddard expressed it, "When we can say 'no,' not only to things that are wrong and sinful, but also to things pleasant, profitable, and good that would hinder and clog our grand duties and our chief work, we shall understand more fully what life is worth, and how to make the most of it."

W. M. Punshon, an English minister, expressed it this way: "All the world over, a double-minded man is unstable in all his ways, like a wave on the streamlet, tossed hither and thither with every eddy of its tide. A determinate purpose in life and a steady adhesion to it through all disadvantages, are indispensable conditions of success."

Decide, once and for all what you want to be, and where you want to go. Robert Thornton, Sr., President of Mercantile National Bank, Dallas, tells me he considers this *the* secret of any success: "The man who has a destination in mind," he says, "may sometimes have to get off the main highway and take a detour. He may have to back up, or circle around, but because he knows where he wants to go, he eventually gets there. The man with no destination in mind never gets back on the main highway, once he must take a detour."

POINTS TO REMEMBER

1. The power in crisis comes to your aid *only* if your decision is to swim instead of sink. Throw a child in water over his head and he will learn to swim in a hurry, *if* he is thinking about swimming, and *if* all his energies are directed toward saving himself. If he is thinking about sinking, he will sink. A crisis can make you or break you, depending upon your own decision, and your own attitude.

2. A true decision "cuts off" all alternatives and channels all your power in one direction. Therefore, when you make a decision, go whole hog and burn your mental bridges behind you.

3. Have you ever really made up your mind to sell with no if's, and's, or but's? If not, you have never used your full selling power.

4. When you make up your mind to sell, give up all care about the outcome and forget the possibility of failure. If you don't want to fail, why use up energy and power considering it? Forget about what you don't want, and concentrate on what you do want. For the time being, at least, act as if it were impossible to fail.

5. Have a long-range goal, then refer small, everyday decisions to that goal. Let the goal decide for you. This way a large amount of energy is saved that you would spend trying to make up your mind.

3

WHAT I'VE LEARNED ABOUT THE POWER SHIFT IN SELLING

AT THE BEGINNING OF THIS BOOK, I SAID THAT the best advice I ever had was given me when that long-distance telephone operator said to me, "Go ahead, sir."

I had made a decision. I had figured out what I wanted to do. Then, at the last minute, with the phone in my hand, I almost changed my mind and called the whole thing off. Why make a fool of myself? After all, it would be better to wait until morning and think some more about it.

When the lady said, "Go ahead!" While the operator was placing the call, last-minute doubts began to creep in. Maybe I wouldn't be able to do it after all, and it would be foolish to try. I came within a hair's breadth of calling the whole thing off. Then the operator's voice came over the phone, saying "Go ahead."

I owe a lot to that operator, and I've often thought what would have happened to me if I had not gone ahead and put my ideas into action. Would I have convinced myself that I was a flop and a failure? Would I have decided that I just couldn't sell anyhow? Probably. And yet, I would have been counting myself out before the bell ever rang for the first round.

I believe there are many salesmen and others today who have a million-dollar bank account of ability, knowledge, and experience but who never write a check on it because they will not act. They've got the power in the motor but will not shift the gears. Power comes only when you shift your gears and get into action.

Wherever you see a person of power, you see a person of action. We often marvel at the power so evident in the lives of the early Christians. They were men of action.

Horace Mann said, "I have never heard anything about the resolutions of the apostles, but a great deal about their acts."

Action Has Power

A beautiful 200-horsepower automobile has no useful power whatsoever so long as the engine idles in neutral. It has tremendous potential power, it is true, but no real power until the gears are shifted and the power of the motor gets into action.

Many salesmen fail not because they do not have sufficient potential horsepower but because they just never seem to "shift into gear." They idle their motors in neutral. There is no power in inactivity. Activity is life. Total inactivity is death.

Passives versus Actives. I have discovered that the real power that comes from shifting your gears is not just that it gives you power in some isolated situation, but that it becomes a habit, a general personality trait, that colors your whole attitude about life.

Psychologist David Seabury has said that the entire human race can be divided into the *actives* and the *passives*. The actives are the people who do things; passives just let things happen. The actives conceive their role in life to be that of an "actor"; the passives conceive their role to be that of a spectator.

If you will go back and read again the Introduction to this book, "Six Hours That Changed My Life," you will see that for 20 years I had all the ear-marks of a passive. I was a member of a church, but not "active"; I belonged to clubs, but took no

active part. When I attended sales meetings and social functions, I never pushed myself, but waited to be called upon.

It's the attitude that counts. The Active personality is forever asking itself, "What can I do about this?"

The Passive personality is forever asking, "What will this do to me?"

The secret of Power in the Active attitude is not that you will be immune from bad breaks or unfortunate circumstances, but in the way you deal with them. Actives *appear* to be more lucky, only because they place themselves in a position to take advantage of luck. As Sophocles pointed out thousands of years ago, "Heaven will not help the man who will not act."

Senator Estes Kefauver, writing in *Reader's Digest* (August 1954), says that his entire success in life is due to the advice given him early in life by his mother, when he returned home from college disheartened and convinced that he was hopeless: "Estes, you must *turn your stumbling blocks* into *stepping stones.* Let hurt feelings be a prod to work just that much harder. If you feel disappointed about your classes, let the disappointment spur you to study more. Then you'll have a triumph to your credit."

The Secret of the Little Black Hen

J. M. "Mack" McGinley, of Dallas, Texas, recently sent me a poem from his famous "scrap book." It illustrates very well the difference between Actives and Passives.

> Said the little Old Red Rooster,
> "Gosh all Hemlock, things are tough;
>   Seems that worms are getting scarcer,
> And I cannot find enough.
>   What's become of all those fat ones
> Is a mystery to me.
>   There were thousands through the rainy spell,
> But now where can they be?"
>
> The Old Black Hen who heard him,
> Didn't grumble or complain;
>   She'd been through lots of dry spells,
> And she'd lived through floods and rain;

> So she flew upon the grindstone,
> And she gave her claws a Whet . . and said:
> "I've never seen the time
> There 'Weren't worms to Get' "

The poem is too long to repeat in its entirety here, but the Little Black Hen began to dig, and the Old Red Rooster sat in the shade and criticized — she was digging in the wrong place — but the hen said, "I must go to the worms — the worms won't come to me." The rooster sat around waiting for another "rainy season" when worms would be plentiful. At the end of the day, the rooster was hungry — and he began to sympathize with the hen "For you're not only hungry, but you must be tired too."

> The Old Black Hen hopped to her perch,
> And she drooped her head in sleep;
> She murmured in a drowsy tone:
> "Young man, hear this and weep . .
> I'm full of worms and happy.
> For I've dined, both long and well;
> The worms were there as always,
> But I had to dig like Hell!"

McGinley adds the postcript:

> Oh, here and there Red Roosters
> Are holding Sales Positions,
> They can't get much business now,
> Because of Poor Conditions.
> But as soon as things get Right Again,
> They'll sell a hundred firms;
> Meanwhile, the Old Black Hens,
> Are out a-gobbling up the Worms.

"Conditions Are Never Right"

There were at least a dozen good reasons why I shouldn't have tried to form an insurance company that night nine years ago. But I decided that the person who waits for "perfect conditions," until he can "see his way clear" all the way to the goal, never acts at all.

For the past 20 years I had been passively waiting for "per-

fect conditions" — waiting for the time when I could see how each obstacle could be overcome. For 20 years these conditions never materialized. Then, with "conditions" at the very lowest ebb they had ever been for me, *I realized my goal in just six hours*; once I got into action, quit vacillating in my own mind over whether I should act or not, and committed myself 100 per cent to going out after what I wanted!

"Conditions" mean everything to the passive personality. He is at the mercy of conditions and circumstances. Like a ship without a rudder, he must go in whichever direction the winds and the currents may take him. This gives him a feeling of helplessness, of being a "victim" of circumstances.

I have come to the conclusion that you can never — or very rarely — see your way clear through to your goal when you first start out. As B. T. Gargus, Manager, Special Life Division, National Banker's Life Insurance Company, said recently in his weekly newsletter:

"Don't worry about what's ahead — go as far as you can see; from there you can see farther."

Actives "Make" Circumstances

Edward Bok wrote a little essay back in 1925 called "You." It is now out of print, but if you can find it in a used-book store, I urge you to get a copy. This little essay came into my hands just when I needed it, for Bok set out in a very inspiring manner the Power that is in the individual man or woman. Among other things, he said this:

Napoleon struck at the very foundation of all this when he said: 'Circumstances? I *make* circumstances.' That was not the word of an egotist. That was fact. We *all* make circumstances. Each one of us.

This set me to thinking: Just exactly what are "circumstances"? If you will give this matter a little thought, I believe you will conclude, as I did, that we all *do* make circumstances. For what we call circumstances are compounded of outside conditions, *plus our own attitudes and actions* about these outside conditions. In a given set of conditions, one man can turn them into favorable circumstances by his own actions; another man may accept them as unfavorable circumstances by his failure to act.

Let me give you a good example:

Summertime Slump—and a "Hot" Salesman

Many life insurance salesmen feel that summertime is an "off season." They can give you all sorts of reasons why it is a bad time to sell. Their reasons are logical and convincing. "Outside conditions" are bad. Passively accepting them, their attitude turns summertime into "unfavorable circumstances" for many salesmen.

Yet, as I write this, Maurice Babby, a relatively newcomer to National Banker's Life Insurance Company, has vaulted into the number-one spot on production. Mr. Babby's sales actually seemed to "get hot" just when the temperature did. I asked A. R. Craig, our Agency Manager, to find out why, and to give the information to our other salesmen. This is what Mr. Craig reported:

Have you ever thought that more money jingles in the pockets of your prospects in the summertime than at any other time of the year, that is, more money free from necessities? In the summer, there is no fuel to buy. There are no school books on the budget. Clothes are less expensive. Your prospect is "family-minded" in the summer. He and his family go hiking and driving together. This is the time to appeal to him on the score of financial protection for his family. His reaction is likely to be more favorable than when his mind is crowded with "rush period" business.

It's an easy habit to get in a "Summer Slump." Its easy to say to yourself, "What's the use of making calls today? Everybody's either on vacation or out for some recreation. I couldn't make any sales anyway." All the time people are living and dying, getting sick, and having accidents. Actually, summer offers the agent a better than even chance to increase his sales because of the "Summer Slump" attitude prevalent among competitors.

It's the Way You "Look at It"

An attitude is a way of "looking at" conditions. Active Personalities are invariably Positive Thinkers. They look at certain conditions and ask, "What are the *advantages;* what can I *do* that will turn some of these liabilities into assets?"

A. R. Craig concluded his analysis of the "Summer Slump" by saying,

If you will adopt the *Right Mental Attitude,* prepare the right kind of selling campaign, and *Keep Driving Forward,* you will find your production for July and August will be just as good as any other time of the year.

So-called physical handicaps can also be turned into assets by an active, affirmative attitude. Charles M. Richey, our District Manager in Chattanooga, Tenn., is 5 feet 4 inches in height. Soon after he got out of college Richey was turned down by a sales manager for a sales job because he was "too short." The sales manager told Richey that six-footers made the best salesmen because they were more impressive.

Richey could have taken this rebuff at face value, hung his head, and given up since there was nothing he could do about his height. But instead, he determined that whatever other people might or might not think about his height he himself would not consider it a handicap, that he would out-sell the six-footers.

When he stopped *thinking* of his height as a handicap, other people were not conscious of it either. When he came to us, I never noticed that he was short, until he himself told me this story. Today, he is the same height, but on the production reports where it counts, he is one of our "tallest" salesmen.

I. D. Jones, our Houston District Manager, is another "shortie" with a long record of high sales. He turns his lack of height into an asset, by addressing his new salesmen like this: "If a little shrimp like me can make a living selling, it ought to prove to you that anybody can sell."

Churchill, Roosevelt, et al

Think of any man or woman you know who has ever accomplished anything at all, and you will discover an *active personality.* Emerson, in explaining the power of Napoleon, said, "Here was a man who in each moment and emergency knew what to do next. . . . Few men have any next; they live from hand to mouth, without plan, and are ever at the end of their line, and after each action wait for an impulse from abroad."

Eisenhower, in writing of his first visit with Churchill and Roosevelt (*Crusade in Europe*) * said, "Tobruk, in the African desert, had just fallen to the Germans and the whole Allied world was thrown into gloom. These two leaders, however, showed no signs of pessimism. It was gratifying to note that they were thinking of *attack* and *victory*, not of defense and defeat."

Hard Work Alone Isn't the Answer

You can't judge Actives and Passives by the amount of hard work they do. I myself had never been lazy. I had always worked hard. But a man can work just as hard *reacting* to life, ducking and dodging, as he can acting upon life. A man on the defensive can wear himself out just as much as a man on the offensive. Actually, a passive, defensive personality can use up more energy, just as an automobile engine can burn just as much gasoline in neutral as it will in "high." Mechanics tell me that the wear and tear on the motor is more damaging when the motor is left idling, and especially if the motor is raced while the gears are in neutral.

There is one difference, however. The Actives are the producers. The amount of energy used up may not be any greater, but they are the only ones to ever "get anywhere." A car in neutral may work as hard as a car in high, but the speedometer reading tells the story; it never "goes places."

Your Actions Determine Your Thoughts

Everyone knows that a man's thoughts determine his actions. But many years ago Psychologist William James pointed out that actions or behavior also have an effect on our thoughts and feelings. The sovereign way to cheerfulness, he said, is to *act cheerful*. Keep acting cheerful, and soon you will begin to *feel* cheerful. Act brave — and in time you will begin to feel

---

* Crusade in Europe (New York: Doubleday, 1948).

brave. The more you run away, the more fearful you become.

I found that when I shifted my gears and changed from *passive* to *active,* it seemed to be a natural thing for my thoughts to become more *positive.* Gradually, I could see a trend towards more *affirmative* attitudes and feelings. It seemed to be almost second nature to think *positively* instead of *negatively.* It seemed that as long as I was involved in "doing," the trend of my thoughts began to take the following course, "What can I *do* about this? What are the things to be *done?*" As long as I was doing nothing, my attitude seemed to be to emphasize all the things that couldn't be done.

I found that as long as I sat passively with my motor in neutral, I couldn't even seem to "see" any good places to go. I looked on the negative. I saw all the bad features in a situation.

But whenever I shifted gears, and once got moving, I could see a lot more things that could be done.

"Do the Thing and You Will Have the Power"

I also discovered, as a lot of other people had before me, that once I started "doing," I seemed to have more power to "do." An automobile cannot start off at 100 miles per hour from a *standing start.* It must first get *moving* and then work up momentum.

I recently had an interesting conversation with John D. Murphy, the magazine writer. His articles have appeared in just about every type of magazine from trade journals to slicks, and on just about every subject matter from farming, sports, personalities, business, psychology. I asked John how he managed to get his ideas, and he said:

I have found that if I sit back and wait for the perfect idea; or wait until I can express an idea correctly, I just never seem to get any ideas worth anything much—or any writing done either. I must *start working* on what there is to work with however unpromising it may appear. It is only after I start writing that ideas come best. As Emerson says, "Do the thing, and you will have the power."

You must step forward. I'm reminded of an incident I saw

not long ago on a city bus, one of those with a treadle that you step down on to open the door. A lady, evidently unfamiliar with the ways of big city buses, stood at the rear door waiting for it to open for her.

"This door will not open," she called out to the driver.

"Step forward, lady," the driver said, "the door will open, but you must step forward."

It seems to me that that is true — not only of buses — but of writing, selling, or anything else. Life is full of closed doors that refuse to open until we "step forward." We must get in motion.

This Practice Will Make You Happier

One of the things you'll learn as you begin to practice being Active instead of Passive is that you'll enjoy life more. Remember, even our Constitution does not guarantee that happiness will come to you but that you have the right to "pursue" it, that is, to get moving and go out after it.

G. Colket Caner, M. D., Associate in Neurology, Massachusetts General Hospital, points out in his fine little book, *It's How You Take It* (New York: Coward-McCann, Inc., 1948), that the one best way to overcome problems and also get satisfaction out of life is to adopt the attitude of "No matter what comes, I can handle it," instead of the fearful attitude, "I hope nothing happens."

"A person who gets a feeling of worth by holding to the idea of *doing what he can* no matter what life brings," says Dr. Caner, "will have inner security. Every difficulty that comes gives the opportunity of meeting it well. His ideal will give him something greater to strive for no matter what success comes his way. It will free him from concern about what others do or don't do, because he will be focusing on carrying on well himself. It will free him from the dread of what fate may bring, because he will take pride in *doing the best he can* no matter what happens. Such an ideal brings happiness and peace of mind by harmonizing the conflicting forces of the personality, making them work together, just as people work together when they have a common goal."

Bonaro and Harry Overstreet, whose insights into human relations have helped thousands, had this to say in one of their lectures:

No one can be deeply and durably happy whose relationship to life is basically *passive* and non-productive: who just lets things happen.

To withhold from the world one's inborn capacities for creative and productive effort is automatically to withhold from one's self a major source of satisfaction and self-respect.

It is also, to put one's self into the vulnerable position of being at the mercy of whatever forces happen to shape one's human and physical environment—and therefore to have all the fears and pent-up hostilities that go with feeling helpless.

POINTS TO REMEMBER

1. Your ability, skill, knowledge, experience, intelligence, personality, are all sources of *potential* sales power. None of them, however, has any actual power until you put them into action. That automobile parked in your driveway has no power whatsoever when it is parked. Read your owner's guide and you will find that it "develops" 200 horse-power only when the motor is turning so many revolutions per minute.

2. Salesmen do not "have" salespower. They *develop* sales power only when they are in action.

3. Passive personalities wait until conditions are right before they act. Conditions are never right, and they never act. Active personalities make conditions right by getting into action.

4. Passive personalities accept various physical and personality handi-caps and do nothing about them. And because they do nothing about them, they are handicaps. Emerson once said that every man's defect could be his greatest strength. Active personalities use their so-called handicaps and turn them into assets.

5. Don't wait until you can see your way clear through to the end of the road before starting out. You can see further down the road only as you travel on it. Don't stand back and wait for doors to open. Step forward, and you will trip the treadle that makes them open.

4

HOW I LEARNED TO HARNESS THE POWER OF SELFISHNESS

ALL MY LIFE I HAD BEEN TAUGHT THAT SELF-ishness was wrong. Then one day I picked up a newspaper and read that Hugh Roy Cullen, the Texas multi-millionaire, known as "The King of the Wildcatters," had just given away another large sum to a charitable institution. When asked why he gave away such large amounts, Mr. Cullen had answered, "because I am a selfish man."

I have since learned, through reading the interesting story of Mr. Cullen's life (Hugh Roy Cullen, *A Story of American Opportunity*),* that this man, who started out in life with only a fourth-grade education has made it possible for millions of students to receive college educations; that he has given away something like $160,000,000 to schools, hospitals, and other charities; that he once gave away $4,000,000 in a single day.

That newspaper story about Hugh Roy Cullen, who had done so much good for others, "because I am a selfish man," started me thinking about selfishness in a new light. I began to see "selfishness" as a powerful instinctive force, that could be used for either good or evil. I came to regard selfishness in somewhat the same light as a powerful wild horse. Let it run

---

* New York: Prentice-Hall, Inc., 1954.

wild and untamed and it can lead you down the road to destruction. But if you learn to break it to the harness, it can as easily pull you down the success road and give others a lift at the same time.

It has been estimated that the system of incentives that our companies built upon this idea has added at least $1,000,000 to our assets. It has also enriched our own workers, given our customers more than they would ever have received otherwise, and resulted in my being able to secure a donation that will exceed $1,000,000 to my own pet charity, The Crippled Children's Foundation of America.

The Two Kinds of Selfishness

If you reduce the word *selfishness* to its simplest definition, it simply means *wanting things for yourself*. Implanted in us by our Creator is a powerful instinctive urge to want things. Without this creative urge, the human race would never have progressed. It drove our forefathers to cross an ocean and brave the perils of a new world. Without this "want power" we would soon die. When our bodies need food, we become hungry and want to eat. This "want power" is behind all accomplishment, even the achievement of a better moral life. For it is generally recognized that no man can change his ways for the better, until he really "wants to."

You can use this power stupidly and ineffectively to *want things* at the expense of others, and without regard for the rights of others. This type of selfishness attempts to get things by depriving other people of them. This is the type of selfishness that has been rightly condemned as "wrong" and that unfortunately has given all selfishness a bad name. There is another type of selfishness. It consists in *wanting things for yourself* that will not harm others, that will not deprive others of any good.

The Power of "Wanting To"

An anti-saloon leaguer is supposed to have once upbraided a drunk in a saloon, "You could stop drinking—if you wanted to."

Whereupon the drunk replied, "I don't doubt that, lady. The only trouble is I don't know how to 'want to.' "

Psychologists now tell us that there is tremendous power in *wanting to*.

The first step in breaking any bad habit is to *want to*.

In an athletic competition, victory often goes to the physically inferior individual or team, who wanted to win.

Recently, I read an account of how a 360-pound man in Atlanta, Georgia, reduced to 180 pounds in six months because he wanted to marry a widow who didn't like fat men. I was interested in this story because it pointed up how "want power" can be much more powerful than "will power."

This man had thought that he wanted to reduce before. But he had other conflicting wants. He wanted to keep on eating tremendous amounts of food. He had tried will power a number of times, but could never stick to his diet.

Then, he met this widow and wanted to marry her more than anything else in the world, but she let it be known she would never marry a fat man. He now had a powerful incentive to reduce. This incentive was so strong that it completely overruled the now insignificant incentive to overeat. And he reduced!

A strong incentive organizes *all* your power toward your goal—by making insignificant any conflicting wants. Perhaps, St. Paul had something like this in mind when he said that he had cast aside the weights that so easily beset him, so that he could run the race before him.

A very strong impelling "want" is the only force that can organize the conflicting lesser "wants."

Many of us, however, cannot really "want" anything with all our might because of false ideas about selfishness. To want anything for yourself is selfish. We have been taught that all selfishness is wrong. The result is what Dr. Karen Horney called putting a general all-inclusive "taboo on wanting anything for ourselves."

We then find ourselves in the position that Douglas E. Lurton describes in his book * *The Power of Positive Living*:

---

* Douglas E. Lurton, *The Power of Positive Living*, New York: McGraw-Hill Book Co., Inc., 1950.

The best things of life are awaiting the grasp of positive people who scorn the negative attitude. The sound fruits of life with their rich juices lie at hand for the taking, and life's best coconuts are up there within reach if we but make positive effort to acquire them.

Often we don't take more of the best fruit simply because of an acquired habit of defeat. We even think it is all right for others to reach out and take their full share, but we hold back when it is our turn. This is a rather ignoble acquiescence. To a large extent it is due primarily to severe limitations we have unwittingly placed upon ourselves.

I might add that to me it is also a rather ignoble concept of our Creator to take the attitude that He doesn't want us to have anything, enjoy anything, or accomplish anything. It is a far cry from the teachings of Jesus, who said, "I came that ye might have life—and have it more abundantly."

Is a general taboo on all selfish wants wise? If we ever became completely unselfish, we would, of course, not have life more abundant; we would die. We would not eat. There would be no point in maintaining our health. By putting a general taboo on our "want power," we cannot really want those things that would benefit us and society anymore than we can want anything else.

Edward J. McGoldrick, Jr., Director of New York City's Bureau of Alcoholic Therapy, has the highest record for successful cures of alcoholics than any individual or any organization. One of Mr. McGoldrick's cardinal principles is to harness the power of selfishness and put it to work *for* the alcoholic instead of *against* him. No real alcoholic is ever cured, he says, because of appeals to his duty to his wife, children, or society. He started drinking for selfish reasons, and he must stop for selfish reasons if he is to stop. He is only cured, says Mr. McGoldrick, when he can see some important personal reason for *wanting* to quit; when he himself wants cure for himself.

Most alcoholics, he says, are selfish in the wrong way. They are selfish in a short-sighted, stupid way. They want what they think is the immediate satisfaction of a drink. They are not selfish enough in wanting other and greater satisfactions that will accrue in the long run from not drinking. It is not enough to tell him that he "ought" to quit. It is not enough for him to try to "will" to quit. It is not enough for him to agree intellectually that there are greater satisfactions. He must see these satisfactions and want them in a selfish personal way.

Speaking of selfishness, he says, "There is no stronger force within us, and it can conduct us to social satisfaction as easily as to self-destruction."

Dr. Karen Horney, who was as much opposed to the stupid, short-sighted antisocial type of selfishness as anyone, said that most of the neurotics who consulted her had lost their power to want anything, and that putting a general taboo against *all* selfishness was perhaps the most antisocial attitude of all. It turns people into neurotics. It frustrates them. Their frustrations bottled up inside them, make them hostile and hard to get along with. And they are never able to develop their powers to their fullest for the benefit of themselves, or society.

So powerful is this ability to "want to" that Dr. Arnold A. Hutschnecker, author of *The Will to Live* *, says that time after time he has seen a person dangerously ill recover when he had some incentive to recover. Dr. Hutschnecker says,

If we truly wish to live, if we have the incentive to live, if we have something to live for—then no matter how sick we may be, no matter how close to death, we do not die. We live, because we want to live.

But the incentive must be one in which we inwardly, utterly believe. It is not the 'everything to live for' in the eyes of the world, which keeps us alive, but the something which meets our own uncompromising measure of what is worth living for.

Just What Is Your Subconscious Mind Like?

It is a well known fact that the subconscious mind is purely selfish. It has to do with our self-preservation, our self-survival, our self-satisfaction. In Asia there is a fishing bird called the cormorant. Natives use it to fish for them by putting a collar around its neck so that it cannot swallow the fish it

* Arnold A. Hutschnecker, M.D., *The Will to Live*. New York: Thomas Y. Crowell Co., 1951.

catches. For a time the bird goes about the business of fishing as usual.

However, it soon stops fishing at all, unless the collar is loosened at intervals so that the bird itself can swallow a fish now and then. The subconscious mind is somewhat like the cormorant. Unless you loosen the collar now and then and allow the subconscious some self-satisfaction, it goes on a sit-down strike. It refuses to work for either you or society.

Personally, I cannot see that this is "wrong" or "evil." If we are made that way, it is because our Creator made us that way, and I for one, give Him credit for knowing what He was doing.

If you will take a look at those areas of the earth where the Buddhist doctrine of "annihilation of all desire" is taught as a religion you will see that society is not benefited by complete unselfishness of the individual. Where the individual is taught to give up all personal desires and wants, you will find that there is more poverty, sickness, and general misery than any-where in the world.

If you take a look at our own country, where the "profit motive" operates, you will find the general population the best cared for and enjoying the highest standard of living anywhere in the world.

We can, of course *use* the power of selfishness in the wrong way. But that will be the subject of another chapter.

How You Can Use the Power of Selfishness

To sell with full power—you must *want* to sell.

And to *want to sell,* you must keep before yourself at all times the *satisfactions* that are to be derived from selling.

As a salesman, you know that prospects often have wants and needs that they do not act upon, simply because they are not sufficiently aware of them. A salesman gets people to act, by turning a spotlight on wants, "bringing home" to the pros-pect all the joys and satisfactions that he will derive if he buys the product. As salesmen, we know that the prospect will not act on these wants until they are shown to him in a very vivid manner. We need to use this same sort of salesmanship on ourselves.

In fact, the only justification at all for salesmanagers is the need to keep salesmen constantly sold on salesmanship. The salesmanager must use the same sort of salesmanship on his salesmen that his salesmen use on prospects.

"Want power" is developed only by incentives, goals, and rewards. If there are no rewards to be had or if the rewards are limited, there is no point in getting ourselves worked up about wanting them.

A. F. Davis, Vice President of The Lincoln Electric Company, Cleveland, Ohio, emphasized this point in telling me how this company started on $200 borrowed capital and rose to be the largest producer of arc welders and welding electrodes in the world.

"Dr. Brooks," he said, "our success is all due to what James F. Lincoln calls 'Intelligent Selfishness.' Our workers wanted higher wages, the company wanted more sales, our customers wanted better and cheaper products. Together with the workers, we worked out a system for satisfying all these wants. Our plant workers today average more than $8,000 per year; they produce up to 12 times as much as workers in comparable plants; we have improved our product and constantly reduced its price; saleswise, we lead the world; and dividends to stockholders have been increased.

"In short, everybody benefited, by what Mr. Lincoln calls 'developing the latent powers that are in every man.' And one of the first steps Mr. Lincoln took toward developing these powers was to remove the limitations on what an 'ordinary plant worker' can earn. The sky is the limit at our company. Some individuals have earned as much as $50,000 in a single year."

Many salesmen seem to forget that the earning capacity of a salesman is limited only by himself. All salesmen already have an "incentive system." The sky is the limit. And in selling either yourself or your salesmen on this, it is better to get down to "cases" with yourself, just as it is better to talk in terms of concrete benefits rather than abstractions to any prospect you are selling.

If you believe it's possible, you can do it. Picture vividly to yourself or to your salesmen the new car, the fine home, the big bank account, and above all the personal satisfaction that is out there waiting for him if he sells. A salesman once told me that I sold him on coming with our company with a very simple remark. His car was about five years old. I looked at it and asked if that was the only car he had. He said it was. Casually, I remarked that most of our boys had current-year models. One of our salesmen who was with me spoke up and said, "Yes, and a good many of them have *two* cars." The prospect inquired around and found this to be true. "When I saw it was possible," he said, "for the first time in my life I found myself really wanting to get out there and sell so I could own one too."

Just as you cannot "move" a prospect until you get him to wanting something he hasn't, you yourself cannot move forward with full steam until you really begin to want something you haven't and realize that your sales effort is the way to get it.

The Best Incentives in the World: How to Use Them

Money can be a powerful incentive to sell, and certainly it must be possible for the salesman to make money if he is to sell. Mr. J. H. Perry, Executive Vice President of one of our companies, has worked out a system of incentives for our salesmen that include profit-sharing bonuses, as well as their regular commissions. It is estimated conservatively that this system of incentives has been worth at least $1,000,000 to our company.

But if incentive is limited only to money rewards, experience has shown this is not enough to develop a man's full powers. For one thing money itself has lost some of its value as a reward. Some companies have found that salesmen will work harder for "merchandise" prizes than for money alone. General Electric upped its sales of electric blankets 40 per cent in the middle of summer by offering "prizes." When the Thor washing machine people put on a big sales contest with lush prizes to winners, the top man sold 265 per cent of his quota and the lowest winner 178 per cent of his quota.

At Nablico we keep sales contests going almost constantly, with guns, radios, electric shavers, and many other items as prizes. If you are a sales manager, I urge you to try this method of offering concrete articles—tangible goods—as prizes.

If you are a salesman, stage your own contest by "promising yourself" that you will use a part of your extra commissions over and above your usual quota to buy yourself some long-cherished luxury item.

Apparently the subconscious mind realizes that it will not derive too much selfish personal satisfaction from earning extra money alone. A large chunk of it will go for taxes. Another large chunk will go for "ordinary living expenses." Perhaps the subconscious knows that the salesman would not spend any extra money to buy himself that $200 shotgun that he *really* wants, anyway, because he would figure it would be "wrong" to spend the money on himself anyway. Keep in mind the tangible satisfactions that a large enough amount of extra money would bring you rather than thinking about only so much dollars and cents.

Mr. Perry worked out numerous other incentives for our salesmen, such as simplifying their paper work and giving them every cooperation in the way of making their work easier and more productive.

What people want most. There is another incentive, however, that is stronger by far than money or even tangible rewards. That is the incentive to "be something" and to "be somebody." This strong basic subconscious urge has spurred man on to develop himself and raise himself above mere animal existence. It is one instinct that man alone of all the animal kingdom has. Like any other instinct, this one can of course be used wrongly, as in the case of a man who commits a crime merely to get his picture in the paper and be recognized by thousands of people. Used rightly—by which I mean sensibly—however, this urge too can be a powerful force for good.

James F. Lincoln, who is conceded to know more about this business of incentives than any other man in America, points out that men will exert themselves to the fullest in amateur athletics where there is no monetary reward at all and where neither safety nor security is an incentive.

"What then," says Mr. Lincoln, "is the incentive that causes people to strive so mightily for success in an amateur athletic game? The answer is *recognition of our abilities by our contemporaries and ourselves*. The gaining by our skills of the feeling that we are a man among men. We sacrifice all other things to this deep satisfaction that comes from proving our competence to ourselves and from knowing that others recognize it. It is the incentive that has made the human race what it is; hence, it is the primary drive on which all successful effort to increase man's efficiency in any human effort must be based. It is our sense of achievement and its recognition by others that we desire most.

Money is of relatively small importance. Money is an economic necessity. Beyond enough for our real needs, money itself is valued less for what it will buy than as an evidence of successful skill in achievement. The man gauges his success by the opinion of those who know his ability and his work. That is what we strive for and we hold all else secondary."

If you who read this are a salesmanager, I urge you publicly to give your men credit for what they do. And do not consider yourself big-hearted or noble when you do. If your men have earned recognition, it belongs to them. Withholding it from them is theft. Nor should you feel that "back patting" or "flattery" is beneath your principles. Honest recognition of work done is not flattery. You want recognition—your salesmen want recognition. Give it to them.

This Plan Helped Us "Beat the Country"

In our companies we have the "President's Club," whose members are the top producers for the month. We have the "Professional Leaguer," the "All Star League," the "Varsity" and many others. When a man makes one of these teams, it is far more than a pat on the back. He knows that he is doing an outstanding job, and he works hard to stay there. In addition to this, a published list of the top producers of all our salesmen goes to each and every salesman, each and every month.

We used this same method when we increased Sunday School attendance at Tyler Street Methodist Church to the highest in all Methodism. Mr. L. H. Graves, Superintendent of the Sunday School, would publicly give credit each Sunday to the class that had increased its membership most. Individuals who had contributed most to the drive were recognized by Mr. Graves, and also frequently by the pastor from the pulpit.

Be generous with credit. If you fail to give people credit, if you fail to give them the recognition that is their due, then you are truly being "selfish" in the most stupid, self-centered sort of way. Douglas E. Lurton tells me that a big survey of workers in some 80 companies disclosed that the chief complaint was not low pay, but rather failure to receive proper credit for work done.

Dr. Ruth E. Barbee tells me that one of the main reasons that so many women "hate housework," and also one of the biggest complaints of wives is that, "It doesn't matter how hard I work, or how much I do, I never get credit for it."

Using the Esteem-Building Principle in Handling Prospects

Your prospects that you call on also want to be "recognized." Mr. T. H. Parham, an associate of mine in the real estate business, once made $300,000 in sales by changing one line in a direct-mail letter. Mr. Parham had originally sent out a mail piece addressed to "Dear Friend." In the form letter he described the homes, gave all the advantages of owning one, and gave the price. The return was so low it hardly paid for the cost of mailing. Then Mr. Parham got an idea.

Addressing a person in a letter as "Dear Friend" does nothing for his self-esteem. He realizes that he is just one of many that is getting the same letter. There is no personal recognition involved at all.

On the next mailing Mr. Parham addressed each letter individually, and started out, "Dear Mr. Smith." He then added one line to the beginning of the letter as follows: "You have been selected to purchase one of these specially located lots for the sum of ———— dollars." That mailing brought in $300,-000 in sales, and Mr. Parham has used the same technique to sell more than $1,000,000 worth of homes by this same method.

Recognize your prospects by making them "special." Make them a "Preferred Prospect." Remember that no woman is interested in a "line" if she thinks "You tell that to all the girls." She wants to be special.

So do prospects.

POINTS TO REMEMBER

1. Selfishness is one of the most powerful forces. Used wrongly, it will bring misery and unhappiness. Harnessed and used correctly, it will provide the steam for your engine to get the things you want and get you where you want to go.

2. Remember that "wanting things" in itself is not wrong. You cannot even achieve a better moral life until you really "want to." Intelligent selfishness has reformed drunkards and enabled the overweight to reduce when all else failed. It has built schools, and hospitals. For example, it has raised wages, increased profits, and lowered the cost to customers in The Lincoln Electric Company. When used rightly, everyone benefits and no one suffers.

3. If you have your "want power" handcuffed and shackled, let it loose and see what it can accomplish for you. Devise your own "Incentive System" and promise yourself certain rewards when you have increased your own sales. Above all, realize that you can sell with power only when you really want to sell.

4. Everyone wants to be somebody. Everybody wants self-esteem. Recognize these selfish wants in other people and see how your human relations improve. Give other people credit for what they do. Show a personal interest in your prospects.

5. Douglas E. Lurton, editor of *Your Life* magazine, says that when he wants something, he asks himself the question, "Is it right?" If the answer to the question is that it will not wrongly deprive others, he then goes after it with full "want power." This is a good rule of thumb in using your own power of selfishness.

5

HOW I DISCOVERED THE POWER OF POSITIVE SELLING

THERE IS A POSITIVE AND NEGATIVE SIDE TO selling. If you have a positive attitude about what salesmanship is and what you are trying to do, you can approach prospects with no inhibitions and with full sales power.

If you have a negative attitude about what salesmanship is, you are likely to be timid and fearful, or, at least, apologetic. Even if you consciously repress these feelings, you will still not be able to bring your full sales power into play.

Your Incentive and Your Job Are Not the Same

What started me thinking along this line was a remark made by James F. Lincoln, head of the Lincoln Electric Company, Cleveland. Mr. Lincoln, you will remember, is the man who asserts that "Intelligent Selfishness" is responsible for the remarkable record at his company, as related in the last chapter.

The remark made by Mr. Lincoln was this: "The *incentive* of business is to make a profit. But the *objective* of business is not to make a profit but to serve a need."

In substance, Mr. Lincoln had said: We get in business because we want to make a profit. And unless we utilize this power of incentive, we cannot use all our own powers. But

what we want, and what our job is, are two different things. We
want a profit. Our workers want higher wages. But our *job*
is making a better and better product that can be sold for less
and less. If we do this job successfully, we'll both get what we
want, and so will our customers.

Now, as a salesman, your *incentive* is to earn a commission.

But getting a commission is not your *job*.

Your *job* is serving the needs of prospects.

And unless you do your job, and do it well, you'll never earn
a commission.

When I fully realized the import of the above, my sales
power increased tremendously.

The Positive and Negative Definition of Salesmanship

Whether you realize it or not, you already have your own
definition of salesmanship in your own mind. The chances are
that you think of your job in one or the other of the two following definitions:

Negative Definition. Salesmanship is a way of getting people
to give me an order, so that I'll get a commission. This is the
definition of the passive salesman who thinks of his job in
terms of only what he'll get out of it. Notice that with this
definition the salesman is almost helpless. Everything depends on the prospect. The salesman is in somewhat the position of a beggar with his hand out. If he is "lucky" or if the
prospect, over whom he has no control, "gives" him something,
he will be successful. No wonder he feels so jittery before
making a call—he is so powerless in the situation.

Positive Definition. The job of the salesman is to serve the
needs of the prospect and help him solve his problems. This
is the definition of the active salesman who is thinking of salesmanship in terms of what he can "do for" the prospect, and
he has a feeling of power because he has the attitude: "Everything depends upon me." His immediate job is to figure out
something he can do that will gain the attention of the prospect, arouse his desire, and help solve one of the prospect's
problems. Nothing in the world can deter him from doing these
things, except himself.

The active salesman approaches the prospect with the attitude: "I've come here to do you a favor. I can help you solve some problem, help you live better, help you enjoy life more."

The passive salesman is apt to go into the sales interview with the negative attitude: "I am asking the prospect to do me a favor." And unless he is a hardened professional beggar, he will be somewhat apologetic and timid in his approach.

Change Your Attitude; Change Your Selling Method

There are always two ways of looking at any situation—the positive and the negative. That night nine years ago I needed money and I wanted money. When I first thought of calling up businessmen and asking them to "give" it to me, I didn't have the nerve.

Then I asked myself why. I saw that I had a negative attitude. Why be apologetic? I had a very good proposition for these men. It was something I had planned and worked on for years. It was an opportunity for *them* as well as for me. I believed it was my opportunity of a lifetime. Then why wouldn't it be their opportunity of a lifetime, too?

The ideal state of your mind when approaching a prospect. When I picked up the telephone that night, I was not a beggar asking for favors. My attitude was, "I have called to offer you the greatest opportunity you ever had in your life." And because this was *my* attitude, they seemed to catch some of the same spirit.

I have heard Dr. Norman Vincent Peale tell how he used this same Power Attitude in selling aluminum ware as a young man. He was so apologetic about asking for orders, so lacking in courage, that he went across the state line where no one would know him.

On his first call, he walked up to a door, rapped on it timidly, and when a housewife demanded, "Well, what do you want?" all he could mutter was, "You don't want any aluminum, do you?"

"Of course not," she said, and slammed the door in his face. The next day he changed his tactics.

He walked boldly up to a door—gave it a confident knock—

and when the door opened, said in a firm voice, "Madam, I have come to sell you something *you need*."

She invited him in, and he got the order.

Pitch Hard Enough and the Bounce Will Take Care of Itself

The salesman's commission and the prospect's needs are tied together. But the only "handle" the salesman can take hold of in this situation is the prospect's needs. It is the only way he can "get at" his commission.

If you saw a man standing before a wall, with a rubber ball on the ground, complaining that the ball would not bounce back to him, you would tell him, "The ball will never bounce until you throw it. You have no direct control over the bounce, but you can control the pitch. And the more power you put into your pitch, the more power there will be in the bounce back."

Many salesmen stand and wait for the bounce-back (commissions) without bothering to put any power in their "pitch" (serving the prospect's needs).

What actually moves a prospect to "bounce back" a commission to the salesman? Is it because the salesman needs the commission? Because he wants it? Because the salesman needs to pay his back rent, or buy his child a pair of shoes? Is it because the salesman is a "nice fellow."

None of these things means anything to the prospect. He is going to part with his money for just one reason—for something the salesman can give him that he would rather have than his money.

The Danger of Dividing Your Selling Power: The Evil of Self-Interest

If this "something" is the controlling factor in the situation, obviously the salesman must concentrate on this something that he can give the customer in exchange for his money. It is a psychological fact that you cannot think of two things at the same time. And if you try, you only divide your power. You cannot be thinking of the prospect's interests and what you can do for him if you are at the same time thinking of your interests and what the prospect can do for you.

W. R. Harris, Vice President and Agency Director, Pinnacle Old Line Insurance Company of Arkansas, is one of the best salesmen I have ever known.

When I asked him his secret, he said, "Well, if I had to boil it all down to just one rule, I would say, 'Think of the customer's profit before your own. Make your presentation in a conscientious way so that the prospect will be impressed with the fact that you have only his interest at heart and want to serve him and his insurance needs.' "

This change in basic attitude about selling gives you power for a number of reasons. First of all, of course, it enables you to give your entire attention and ability to the *one thing* that will result in a sale: The prospect: his needs, his wants, his interests.

But it also gives you new power in every phase of selling. We have already seen how it can give you more courage and confidence in your approach. You will also discover that it will give you more power in your close without your giving any thought to the matter.

If you operate upon the premise that salesmanship is a method of getting something away from the prospect, all your behavior will be consistent with that premise. If you are a decent person who has been taught that it is wrong to take things way from people, there will be some degree of guilt about selling.

You will be timid and apologetic about selling and never realize why. You will find it difficult to close, simply because you may not have the heart to go through with it. If you regard salesmanship as a "contest" in which you win over the prospect, your conscience may get the better of you when it seems time to "move in for the kill." You will find it difficult to "go all out" and use all your power, for the same reason. You may kill time and think up excuses to keep from getting down to work, without ever realizing that your conscience is to blame.

When you begin to see salesmanship as an opportunity for

doing things for people, all this changes. Personally, I would never try to sell anything that I was not firmly convinced would benefit the buyer.

And unless you yourself actually believe that what you are selling is going to benefit your customers, you have no business selling it. Come to a decision about the matter once and for all. If you have a legitimate reason for selling, if your product or service will benefit the prospect, if you have something to offer him, then stop being apologetic about it and go all out.

On the other hand, if you haven't anything to offer, if your product or service really is something you should feel guilty about palming off on people, then stop trying to "half-sell" it and stop trying to sell it altogether.

The stupidity of "What's in it for me?" Henry J. Kaiser has said, "An ingrained attitude of 'What will I get out of it?' leads up a blind alley to failure. In a job, business, or profession, you are simply filling human wants. You get ahead in direct relation to how well you offer the toil or services or brains that others want and will pay for."

Keep These Points in Mind

1. A salesman is not a beggar. Don't go out with the attitude that the prospect owes you anything, or that your success depends upon his "giving" you something.

2. A salesman is not a thief. No salesman need feel guilty about his job if he is a legitimate salesman. Salesmen are the spark plugs of our economy and help the entire economic structure as well as the individual.

3. A salesman is a servant. Concentrate on what you can do for the prospect. Look for needs that your product or service can serve.

6

THE POWER OF BELIEF AND WHAT IT WILL DO FOR YOU

THIS CHAPTER CONTAINS ONE OF THE MOST important secrets of POWER SELLING.

Using it, a young man, with no previous selling experience, earned $12,000 in one year, selling door-to-door with no leads and in a country where he couldn't even speak the language!

Another salesman who was on the verge of giving up selling altogether, hit upon this secret accidentally, and quickly sold $100,000 of his product.

An office worker, stepped into selling "cold," used this key, and became one of the most successful salesmen in his organization.

Sell Your First Prospect

I sometimes tell our salesmen: "If you can sell your first prospect every morning, I can guarantee that you will imbue yourself with a sales power that will last throughout the entire day, and enable you to sell better than you have ever sold before."

To convince the other fellow, first convince yourself. This all important prospect is not the first man or woman you call upon, it is the prospect you see in your own bathroom mirror.

48

Sell this man in your bathroom mirror. Sell him on the idea that you have a fine product or service; sell him on the idea that you are going to sell like you never sold before; sell him the idea that your Creator equipped you for success; sell him the idea that you *can do it,* and your success as a salesman is assured.

A demonstration of the power of belief. Recently, I was in Los Angeles for a month, where I had been asked by Chapman College to assist in setting up their School of Business Administration and to prepare a course in salesmanship. One evening, psychology professor Melvin Powers invited me to go with him to see a demonstration in hypnosis.

A young 200-pound man was hypnotized and told by the hypnotist that he could not rise from his chair. The young man struggled and strained until you could see his muscles standing out like cords, but he could not rise from that chair. Then the hypnotist placed an ordinary pencil on a table and told the subject that it weighed 500 pounds and that he could not lift it. Again, he struggled and strained, but the pencil did not budge from the table!

Next, he took a rather frail-looking young man, hypnotized him, and told him that he was a strong man. He then had this young man stretch out his body with the back of his head resting on one chair, and his heels on the other. Two men then sat upon his chest and midsection, and he supported them with the greatest of ease.

Next, a timid, obviously self-conscious man was selected. The hypnotist told him he was a great orator, and he proceeded to speak in the most poised, self-assured manner I have even seen.

"What is the meaning of this?" I asked Professor Powers. Is this all a fake, or is he using some mysterious power over these people, or what?"

"No, Pierce," he said, "it is not a fake. And the hypnotist has no power at all. *The power is all inside the subjects.* I wanted you to see this because of your interest in salesmanship and the power of belief. What has happened is that the hypnotist has placed them in a position where he has their entire attention. Their attention is not divided among conflicting ideas. They only pay attention to what the hypnotist tells them. If you salesmen could ever get the 100 per cent attention of your prospects, they would believe you 100 per cent and would buy your products.

"But even more important," he went on, "if you salesmen would sell yourselves the idea that you *can* sell and that you are *going to sell*, the results would probably be just as amazing as those you have witnessed here tonight. For, in simple language, that is all that this hypnotist has been doing. He *sold* the athlete the idea that he could not lift the pencil. He *sold* the frail young man the idea he could support several hundred pounds. *Their own belief* was the power that kept the one from being able to lift a pencil and enabled the other to lift a weight far heavier than he had ever lifted before.

"What you have seen here tonight is not something mysterious. You have merely seen in an exaggerated form a psychological law that all of us use every day. All of us are continually 'selling' ourselves ideas that 'I can't do that' or 'I can do such and such.'

"Not only that," continued Professor Powers, "our own beliefs color the beliefs of other people. Beliefs are catching. If you *really* believe a thing yourself, your belief gets across to the other person. If you really believe in the product you're selling, it's easy to convince the prospect."

From Failure to a $100,000 Sale

I immediately thought of an incident that had happened several years ago when I was affiliated with a company that had the distributorship for an automobile battery rejuvenator. The product was a small tablet that you dropped into your battery when you found your battery "run down." After a few minutes the rejuvenator got enough pep into the battery to enable you to get to the nearest service station where you could have your battery properly charged. I remembered a young salesman, "Windy" Adams. "Windy" was about ready to give up selling.

"I'm not having much luck," Dr. Brooks," he said. "I guess I'm just not cut out for a salesman."

He assured me that he "believed in the product." We had all sorts of literature proving that the tablets really did the job they were supposed to do. I encouraged him to stick it out a little longer.

A few weeks later I saw "Windy" again. He was a changed man. I had noticed with interest that his sales had been sky-rocketing. "What's happened to you, "Windy"?" I asked.

"Dr. Brooks," he said, "this thing really works! I was out in the country the other day and left my parking lights on. When I came back to my car, the battery wouldn't turn the motor. I thought of the sample tablets I had with me and dropped one in each cell of the battery. I waited 15 minutes like the instructions say and tried my starter. The darn thing worked just like they said it would."

"But I don't understand," I said, "You told me two weeks ago you believed in the product. Why all this sudden enthusiasm when you find it works?"

"Well, Dr. Brooks," he said, "I did believe it in a way, but now I *really believe it.*"

And this man, who *thought* he believed in his product and was a failure then found he *really* believed in it and went on to sell $100,000 worth of his product within the next six months.

Believe in Your Salesmen

If you're a salesmanager, believe in your salesmen. If you have a man you can't believe in, do both yourself and him a favor by firing him. Criticism is often necessary. The salesmanager sees a mistake that needs correcting. The only way to get it corrected is to bring it to the salesman's attention. But it is important that criticism be given in the proper spirit. Never let a salesman get the idea that you don't believe in *him.* As long as a salesman knows you believe in *him,* you can criticize his *methods* and he'll take it in his stride.

Let me give you a good example. Sidney Osterhout, our District Manager in Columbia, S.C. once had a serious slump in his organization. As Sidney himself tells it,

The attitude of defeat was contagious and nothing seemed to work. I tried contests, I scolded, I criticised, I implored—yet nothing seemed to help. Then one day I happened to meet an old retired Marine Colonel, and being an ex-Marine myself, we naturally got to talking about different organizations. He went on to point out the method and means of producing enthusiasm in such a great organization as the U.S. Marine Corps and said they could probably be applied to any group. This gave me a chance to bring up the trouble I was having with morale in my own organization and how discouraged I was.

'Well,' he said, 'Remember when you were in the Marines. Remember basic training? If you made a mistake, it was brought to your attention in no uncertain terms. There was no glossing over, no pretty words. But you didn't mind and it didn't get you down because at the same time everyone in the organization was selling you the idea that you were the best in the land—one of America's finest. Remember the definition of morale: I'm the best doggoned soldier, in the best doggoned squad, in the best platoon, etc.? You felt proud of yourself because you knew that your officers believed in you. They kept selling you the idea that a Marine is the best there is. They believed in you and you believed in yourself.'

'Well,' says Sidney, 'I did remember the feeling of self-confidence and sureness and self-pride I had when I had been in the Marines, and I determined I would instill this same morale in my men by letting them know I believed in them. In our District sales meeting the next week I applied these tactics. I immediately saw the reaction before the meeting ended that day. We went on to have one of our most outstanding months in cost and production, and today we take a lot of pride in our sales force and the cocky self-assurance the men have all seemed to develop since that time.

This Made a Man President of His Company

When I started to write this book, I asked my friend L. H. Graves, Jr., a great salesman and organizer, to give me some material from his own remarkable career. Today he is president of Nebraska Life Insurance Company and Executive Vice President of National Banker's Life.

When I first started selling, after I had been working for years in an office," he said, "my first problem was to become confident of my ability to sell. I worked on myself harder than I have ever worked on any prospect since. I knew I had to sell myself confidence.

"I went about it in a methodical way, just as I would sell any other prospect. I knew I had to condition my own mind before I could do anything. So, I kept giving myself sales talks, then going out and making actual calls, going ahead and calling on the people I had been afraid to contact. Soon my self assurance had developed to the point that I felt like taking on even tougher customers. I kept using this combination to enable me to tackle tougher and tougher jobs and do the things I had been afraid to do. First, I'd sell myself the idea I could do it, then I'd go out and tackle the job. When I actually did the thing I had been afraid to do, it 'backed up' my sales talk and gave me the confidence to try something a little more difficult.

Confidence and Loyalty were my two key words," he said. I made up my mind that I would sell myself confidence; that I would never work for a company that I could not be 100 per cent loyal to; or sell a product I did not believe in. If you feel that you cannot wholeheartedly believe in your company or if you feel apologetic about it, this feeling unconsciously detracts from your sales power. You cannot force yourself to go 'all out.' To me, this loyalty is more than a matter of ethics; it has a definite dollars and cents value.

H. V. Kaltenborn's Selling Secret

When H. V. Kaltenborn was a young man he decided he wanted to learn about the peoples of the world first hand. The first country he visited was France. For a year he supported himself selling stereo viewers and slides, forerunners to our 3-D pictures today. Kaltenborn could not speak French. He had no previous selling experience. He did all his selling "cold," door-to-door.

He got a Frenchman to write out his sales talk in French, memorized it, and repeated it until he could make himself understood. He stuck this written-out sales talk in his hat band; and if he had difficulty in making himself understood, he simply pointed to the written pitch and let them read for themselves.

How could anyone hope to sell by such crude methods?

Kaltenborn not only supported himself for a year, he left with $12,000 cash! His one asset was that he believed he could do it.

"I gave myself little pep talks every morning," he says. "I convinced myself I was going to sell, and I worked myself up to such a pitch of enthusiasm that I could hardly wait to get out and begin selling."

"Sell yourself." Here is the way some of our own top producers do it: G. L. Meyers says,

When I leave home every morning to go out in the field of selling, I keep telling myself that I am sure that I will convince several people that day to buy from me. I have found that a salesman is limited by his own thoughts. There are no bounds in selling, and a salesman's earnings are limited to his own desires.

Turner Carpenter, Jr.:

Every morning I give thanks for the new day and the new opportunities waiting for me. I think of my prospects and resolve to do something that will help them, whether they buy or not. I've found it helps to affirm aloud that I am going to have a great day.

R. C. King, our Manager of Sales for East Texas, had this to say,

In making a sale, I always expect the prospect to have the same confidence in me that I have in myself. I have proved to myself that self-confidence and the ability to make others have the same confidence in me, without making them think of me as a boastful fellow, are the most outstanding assets any salesman can have. Therefore when things aren't going right, I have a heart-to-heart talk with myself and usually find I need to do some more selling on myself.

"It Can Be Done"

The first step toward using your own power of belief is to realize first of all that the job itself "can be done." The desired goal must be regarded as a "possibility" before you can begin to think whether or not you can do it.

Have you ever wondered why it is that for thousands of years no man ever ran the mile in four minutes? Yet, within one month after Roger Bannister ran the mile in 3:59.4 on May 6, 1954, the former world's record was beaten three times, and two months later, Bannister's own new record was bettered by John Landy.

Red Smith, the famous sports writer, says it is not because

runners have suddenly developed new physical power, but because a mental barrier has been removed. For years, men believed it was humanly impossible for a man to run a mile in four minutes or less. And for years no man did. They got within fractions of a second of the magic mark, but until Bannister cracked the mental barrier in 1954, none of them ever did it. Red Smith predicts that more and more runners will run the mile in four minutes or less, now that it has become accepted that such a thing is humanly possible, or "it can be done."

What is your own "mental quota?" All of us have our own mental barriers — our own individual "quotas" of what we conceive "can be done" in the way of selling. Perhaps you do not realize that you have such an individual mental "quota," but a little reflection will convince you that you have. No salesman ever exceeds his own mental barrier, or what he secretly believes "can be done." He can work himself to death, but he still will not exceed his own preconceived "quota" unless he himself raises his quota or enlarges the area of what he considers to be "possible."

J. George Frederick, founder of the New York Sales Managers' Club, once told about a certain salesman who "thought of himself as a $10,000 a year man." This salesman was working in a lush territory and earning for himself $10,000. His territory was reduced by 25 per cent and he still made $10,000. The next year it was cut in half and he still made $10,000. Finally, his territory was reduced to only one-quarter of its original size. Yet, he continued to make $10,000 per year. This man made his own "quota" regardless of outside conditions. Yet, when he had a rich "easy" territory, he found it impossible to do any better than when he had a "poor" territory.

Before you even begin to unlock your powers to accomplish any goal, you must begin thinking of the goal in terms of it's being "possible."

Believing That It Is "Possible" Built the Largest Sunday School

We also used this same technique to increase Sunday School attendance at Tyler Street Methodist Church. At the beginning of our "drive," attendance was running around 1,000.

The goal was set at an increase of from 100 to 200. This was the "possibilities" that we were thinking of.

However, in meetings with the pastor, membership committee, and other groups, we began to "raise our sights." What caused us to raise our sights was the discovery that the national record was 1,685 average attendance for three months time, on a quarterly basis. We had a mass meeting of the entire group of workers, teachers, and officials and decided, "This is what we are going to do ——." From our "drive" we had already increased membership to around 1,200, which we had thought of as our "limit." But when we learned that the national record was only a few more hundreds, we began to consider for the first time the possibilities of our setting a record. We would set our goal at 1,500 and achieve perhaps 1,300 or 1,400. Then, we would set the goal a little higher and increase membership a little more. Finally, we did set a new record of 1,700 average attendance which still stands as the largest average Sunday school attendance in Methodism.

Four words that saved a man from failure. Jim Partain, one of our District Managers, says that these four little words, "It can be done," saved him from failure as a salesman.

He had been with us a period of six months and "I had accomplished everything but success," he says. "In fact, I considered myself a successful failure. After conferring with Mr. John W. Richey, my State Manager, I admitted that his faith in me was unfounded, and to save him further embarrassment I would resign. But Mr. Richey saw more in me than I saw in myself, and told me to report to another office for a conference with Mr. Sam Campbell. Words cannot express the knowledge I gained from these meetings.

"I got myself off in a corner and just started *selling myself*. If these successful men were so sure I could be successful, then 'It could be done.' That was the clincher. I adopted a little slogan: 'It can be done!' I made this slogan synonymous with my work. When anything came up that seemed hard or out of reason, I'd just remind myself that 'It Can Be Done.' Sure enough, in most cases my problems were negligible."

Jim perhaps didn't know it, but he had borrowed the sales secret of one of America's most successful salesmen and businessmen. Philip D. Wagoner, Chairman of the Board, Underwood Corporation, early in his career read Peter B. Kyne's story "The Go-Getter."

You may remember that the hero of this story was given an "impossible" assignment to secure a certain blue vase. The cards were stacked against him deliberately. All sorts of obstacles were planned and put in his path. But he kept to his determination that "It Can Be Done" and in the end got the vase.

Several years ago the All-Star Salesmen of Underwood Corporation presented Mr. Wagoner with a signet ring bearing a replica of the blue vase, symbolizing his philosophy of "It Can Be Done."

You Must Believe in Yourself

The next step to using the power of belief is to have enough belief in yourself to believe that "You can do it." Belief in yourself means more than the mere intellectual recognition that you have certain aptitudes and abilities that equip you for the job. It means also having the *feeling* that you have a "right" to do it. The person with an inferiority complex cuts himself off from his power, not because he thinks he does not have basic ability, but because he feels he has no "right" to use it. People would think him presumptuous. He "knows" that his ideas are good, yet he would be ashamed to get up and voice them. The attitude that shuts him off from his power is not so much "I cannot," but rather the feeling, "I may not."

On the other hand, we all know from our associations with others, and perhaps from bitter personal experience, that nothing can rob us of power, and make us miserable in the bargain, so much as taking ourselves too seriously, putting too much stock in our own self-importance.

Dr. Norman Vincent Peale helped clear up this dilemma for me in a speech I heard him make. In substance, Dr. Peale said something like this: Man needs to feel important. He needs a sense of dignity and self-respect. Man needs to believe in himself. But we can achieve this belief in ourselves only when we realize that man is important, not in himself as a separate personality standing alone, but that Man is important because of his relationship to his Creator.

It depends upon which way you are looking whether belief in yourself is a curse or a blessing. If you get the idea that you, John Doe, are important because you *are* John Doe and because of the great things that *you* have done and can do, then you are headed for unhappiness and failure. But if you can see that you, John Doe, are not very important by yourself but that you are a child of God, that He made you and put you here for a purpose, and that you are important *as His instrument,* then belief in yourself is a blessing.

An electric light bulb, as a thing in itself isn't worth much. It has no power. It cannot make any light. Plug it into a socket, however, and it becomes terribly important. It can light your room. The bulb shines, but the real power comes from a dynamo many miles away. We say that the bulb *brings* light into our room, which it does. But the light *came* from a dynamo, which only uses the bulb as a channel of expression.

In this book, I am trying to tell you how POWER SELLING brought me success. But, I am convinced that whatever success I have had really came from my Creator. Realizing this was one of the greatest discoveries I ever made.

To me, it all boils down to the fact that a man cannot really believe in himself unless he believes in his Creator. You may be a small cog in the scheme of things. Perhaps that small cog is not worth very much all by itself. But if you can get the picture, the over-all importance of the entire scheme, then that small cog is of tremendous worth and importance.

I also cannot see how a man can have much belief in himself unless he believes in mankind. People who deprecate the human race and who attempt to convince themselves that they are "better" than other people, never seem to have much self-confidence deep down where it counts. I cannot see how they can.

As I see it, our only justification for feeling that we have some personal worth and dignity, is that a wise and perfect Creator made us. If we really believe in this Creator, then we must believe in His creations. We would think a man insane who told us in one breath that a certain artist was the world's best and most perfect artist; then told us in the next breath, that all his pictures were sorry, miserable worthless junk. But if we believe in ourselves for this reason, we must believe in all other men, for the same reason.

I believe that every man was created for success. Not all of us were created for the same success. But I cannot conceive of a wise and perfect Creator creating a product that He meant to be a failure.

POINTS TO REMEMBER

1. You can't go all out to accomplish something you feel is impossible. Your subconscious mind goes on a strike if you are convinced that what you are trying to do is impossible. After all, why try at all, if the effort is sure to be wasted. Transfer your goal from the "impossible" to the "possible" category and new power seems to spring to your aid.

2. You do not require sure *knowledge* that you are *certain* to succeed in order to tap this power. All that is needed is the *faith* that the thing *is* possible and that "it *can* be done." Thinking of your goal as a possibility is the first step toward reaching it.

3. In order really to believe in yourself, you must believe in your Creator.

4. In order really to believe in yourself, you must believe in other people.

5. If you "really believe" in your product, you can sell it. There is a difference, however, in "thinking" you believe in it, and really believing in it.

7

YOU CAN'T GO WRONG—
IF YOU SELL IT RIGHT

MIRABEAU ONCE SAID, "IF HONESTY DID NOT exist, we ought to invent it as the best means of getting rich."

This is not a chapter about "How to Stay within the Law." Very few salesmen are dishonest in the sense of deliberately swindling the customer. The old "gold brick" salesmen have just about disappeared from the scene. I am speaking about a subtler form of dishonesty: exaggeration, overstatement, promising by implication more than you can deliver, and failure to tell the whole truth. Using technical, fine-print language that the prospect doesn't understand comes in this category, as do all types of evasion.

The dishonest salesman hurts himself more than anyone else. The greatest asset any salesman can have is to be believed. If prospects feel they can believe you and trust you, they will buy from you. But once word gets around that you are a bunk artist, you might as well give up.

Sincerity Is Power

The sincere salesman inspires confidence in the people he contacts. Prospects feel *safe* with him. They feel they can trust him. They allow him to get inside their defenses.

But you cannot get this valuable power by merely saying to yourself, "O.K. Sincerity is a good thing. I will act more sincerely from here on."

Trying hard to appear sincere can inspire distrust. The prospect senses that you are putting on an act. What you really think gets across to the prospect in your manner, the look on your face, the tone of your voice, and a hundred other ways that you are not aware of and cannot cover up. You cannot be sincere if you are attempting to sell a product that you do not believe in.

On the other hand, if you are sincere, if you really believe that your product or service is worth while and needs no apology, you don't have to worry about getting your sincerity across. There is just one way to be sincere, and that is really to believe what you are saying and to tell the truth at all times.

Five Top Salesmen Tell Their Sales Secrets

When I started planning this book, I asked a number of highly successful salesmen I knew and was associated with to write me, in a few words, their "one big sales secret." I was impressed by the number who answered that simple honesty was the best sales secret of all.

For example: Joe A. Jennings, President of Pinnacle Old Line Insurance Company, Little Rock, Arkansas, told me,

My constant motto, repeated every morning before I start to work, is as follows: 'No wealth or position can long endure unless it is built on Truth and Justice; therefore, I will engage in no transaction that does not benefit those whom it affects.

Robert L. Hill, former Industrial Accident Commissioner for the State of Texas and now head of our highly successful Guaranty Mortgage Company:

Sincerity is the key to any success. Honesty, above all, in everything you do. Just a glance above, and that good feeling within your heart will let you know it is honest.

Wade Hudnall, one of our oldest top producers, from Austin, Texas:

Since people must believe and depend upon your statements, honesty in selling is what gives you power to close.

W. Frank Simmons, District Manager, Durham, N. C.:

To gain the confidence of your clientele, you must be sincere in your sales talk and you must be equally sincere in rendering service afterward. *'Sell it Right'* whatever your wares may be has always been our motto.

M. B. "Pat" Tobin, our District Manager for North Louisiana:

My success as a salesman really began when I took Christ as my helper. To me, this means relieving myself of many worries, being able to substitute faith for fear, and, of course, that I must be scrupulously honest and truthful in all my dealings.

In my time I have seen many salesmen come and go. I have seen small-time salesmen, out to make a fast-buck, by hoodwinking the prospect into buying their products. Without exception, these men, who are really not "salesmen" at all because they never used real salesmanship to make a sale, always disappear from the scene and are forgotten.

On the other hand, I have seen many salesmen rise to the top and stay there. Again, without exception, I have never known one of these top-notchers who did not have a reputation for telling the truth.

Why "Bunk Artists" Can't Be Power Salesmen

To sell with power, a salesman must sell with his heart, as well as with his head. He must put his whole heart and soul into his sales-pitch. No one can "put everything he's got" into a sales pitch if, in the back of his mind, he himself does not believe what he is saying. Science has demonstrated, through the lie-detector, that we are not the same physically when we tell a lie as we are when we tell the truth. Our heart, breathing, our sweat glands, even our brain, act in an abnormal manner.

"If You Can Sleep at Night, You Can Sell!"

My father told me many years ago that one of the greatest

factors in success is that you must be "sure of your conscience."
It was his belief that the greatest drawback to a man's powers
was his own bad conscience. Only if you are sure in your own
mind that your course is honest and "right," can you go all out
and turn on full power in presenting your proposition. If you
know that you are misrepresenting facts or gypping the customer, you adopt an apologetic, timid, and evasive approach,
unless you are a hardened, professional criminal.

I remember one instance when my own insurance company
was young, and I was anxious to get some big policies. I was
trying to sell one of those fabled Texans who is so rich that he
can afford to throw away his Cadillac when the ash trays get
full.

After several visits in which I had put everything I had
into trying to sell him, it looked as if he was about ready to
sign on the dotted line.

With pen in his hand, he said to me, "By the way, I fly my
own plane quite a bit. If I'm killed flying my plane this policy
will pay double indemnity just the same, won't it?"

I saw my hopes of a big sale fading away. The chances
were this man would never have read his policy after he
received it.

I was disheartened, for I had been sure I was going to close
the sale, but I said, "No, this policy will not cover that, and I
did not know you flew your own plane or I would have mentioned it to you."

He hesitated for just a minute, then said, "Oh well, I'll take
it anyway."

During the next 30 days, he took the initiative in introduc-
ing me to three of his wealthy friends, and each time, told
them, "You can depend upon whatever he tells you." I ended
up selling each of the three a nice-sized policy.

On another occasion, I remember trying to sell a $40,000
house to a widow. She liked the house, and she appeared to
have great confidence in everything I told her. Finally, she
said to me, "Dr. Brooks, I would like some advice. I like
this house; in fact it is what I've always dreamed of. But, I
have only $10,000 left of my insurance money. I could put

this down as a down-payment, and rent out a couple of rooms to friends of mine and have enough to meet the monthly payments. I have a job that pays me just enough to live on. Do you think I can afford to buy this house?

"No," I said, "I certainly don't think you can, and I believe that you would be foolish to try." I didn't sell the widow any kind of house. But she told the story to everyone she knew. I sold a number of houses to people who said to me, "I heard about the real estate salesman who advised the widow *not to buy* a house."

Vincent Riggio was an immigrant who came to this country in 1883 as a small boy. At 13 he had to quit school and go to work. He worked in a tailor shop and later became a barber. One day a customer, who was sales manager for a tobacco company told him he ought to try selling.

Riggio tried selling and was such a success at it that he was district manager for the company within a year. He broke all selling records in the history of his company. In 1929 he was made Vice President of The American Tobacco Company in charge of sales. From there he went on to become president.

When someone asked Riggio the secret of salesmanship, he said, "Work hard, use common sense, and *always speak the truth.*"

Are You Honest With Yourself?

All my life, I tried to be honest in my dealings with other people. But I must confess that I have not always been honest with myself.

When I had that little heart-to-heart talk with myself that night, I could see that I had often been downright dishonest with myself. Let me give you some examples:

If conscience told me I was not accomplishing all that I could, I misrepresented facts to myself and told myself that I was, after all, doing about all that I could to get on.

If I failed to make a sale or had a bad month, I excused myself by placing the blame on everything else except myself. It was the time of the year. People just weren't buying. Times were bad, etc., etc.

I frequently wasted my own time piddling around kidding myself that I was "planning" or "waiting for the right moment."

I was not honest with myself by not putting everything I had into my sales pitch.

Lying to yourself (we call it *rationalizing*) and cheating yourself are just as immoral as cheating others. And the results of this personal dishonesty can be disastrous.

A psychologist explains why self-deception robs you of power. The late Dr. Karen Horney said that a man "cannot develop his full human potentialities unless he is truthful to himself; unless he is active and productive; unless he relates himself to others in the spirit of mutuality." *

Dr. Horney stated that many people rob themselves of their powers by building up in their imaginations an "idealized self," which possesses all the attributes they would like to have. This idealized self is perfect in every way. It is powerful, successful, never makes mistakes, is always right, and so on.

To have an ideal is fine. But trouble starts when the individual starts to kid himself that he *is* this idealized self. He then uses up half his power trying to maintain the pretense and trying to keep himself or anyone else from having to face up to the fact that he is not his idealized self. A person comes to believe this delusion by being dishonest with himself.

"There are endless ways in which he disregards evidence that he does not choose to see. He forgets; it does not count; it was accidental; it was on account of circumstances or because others provoked him; he couldn't help it because it was 'natural.' Like a fraudulent bookkeeper, he goes to any length to maintain the double account; but, unlike him, he credits himself only with the favorable one and professes ignorance of the other."

The salesman's occupational failing. Salesmen are especially prone to this sort of self-deception. A salesman may not be selling because he is spending too much time sitting on the seat of his pants. But he will not admit this. He is merely in a "slump."

---

* Dr. Karen Horney, *Neurosis and Human Growth*, New York: W. W. Norton & Company, Inc., 1950.

The chances are you have never heard a salesman say, "I'm not selling well anymore. It's because I'm too lazy."

Instead he says, "I'm in a slump." This enables him to kid himself that he is still a top-notch salesman who is merely in a slump. The slump, he will tell you, is caused by business conditions, the fact that his wife nags him, or any number of other things except the truth, which is that he is not getting out seeing prospects and selling them. Until he is honest enough to admit to himself that he just isn't seeing enough prospects or selling hard enough, he won't do anything to improve himself.

When the sales are few and far between, another way that salesmen are able to kid themselves along that they are super-salesmen is the "bull session." The order book may show that they are flops as salesmen, but they can still be "big shots" in the bull session.

I used to be addicted to these office bull sessions myself. I still like to meet salesmen in the evening and talk shop and swap experiences. But I no longer use the bull session as a substitute for real honest-to-goodness sales accomplishment.

One of the good things that happened to me in 1945 was that I was forced to admit the truth to myself about myself. One of the things I saw was that I had tried to use an imaginative success as a substitute for real accomplishment. I saw that my talking about selling, was just a substitute for real selling. For 20 years I had talked about the things I was going to do "someday." Perhaps this was one of the reasons I never went out and actually did them. I got too much satisfaction out of talking about it.

One of the first things I did was to go out and buy me a picture of two raggedy old bums. Perhaps you have seen a copy of it. One hobo has obviously been telling the other hobo of some exploit or offering some advice. The caption under the picture says, "If you're so damn smart, why ain't you rich?" The picture still hangs on my office wall, as a constant reminder that *talking* about selling isn't the same as *selling*.

The value of a little soul-searching. Now, when things go

wrong with me, when things don't work out right, I remember that night back in 1945, and I go off alone to have a little heart-to-heart talk with myself. In these little talks I try to be just as honest with myself as I can. What caused the trouble in this situation? Was I too bull-headed? Did I expect too much of the other fellow? Was my ego or pride hurt?

Nobody likes to admit mistakes, even to himself. Very few of us find it easy to admit to ourselves that we have had our pride hurt, that we have been too egotistical, that we have been selfish or lazy, or that we have lost our temper without cause. But we are all capable of each of these things from time to time. When we are, attempts to find excuses or to cover up to ourselves by placing the blame elsewhere never gets us out of the trouble.

The first step toward correcting a fault is to admit to yourself that you have it. Then you can deal with it. "Honest confession is good for the soul," even if it may be rough on the ego. We have new power over our shortcomings once we admit them and begin to deal with them as realities.

Another thing most of us hate to admit to ourselves is fear. And because we won't admit to ourselves that we *are* afraid, we have no way of dealing with the fear. Frank Bettger, in his book, *How I Raised Myself from Failure to Success in Selling* * tells how he never did learn to control fear until he found the courage to admit his fear. "When you're afraid, admit it," he says. Strangely enough if you don't try to cover up your fear from yourself or others, your fear will likely vanish.

I once knew a man who had a so-called "uncontrollable" temper. He made his own life and that of his associates miserable from time to time by wild outbursts. He was always "sorry," and made all sorts of excuses for himself.

"I just can't help it," he would say, "I was just born with a high temper," or, "I try hard to control my temper, but I just can't."

Then one day he met a girl and decided he wanted to marry

---

* New York: Prentice-Hall, Inc., 1949.

her. Everything went smoothly until he had one of his "uncontrollable" tantrums.

"I'm sorry," he said, "I was born with an uncontrollable temper and I can't do anything about it."

"No," she said to him, "you are not telling the truth. The truth is that you are a vain, egotistical man, who somehow thinks he is entitled to being treated with kid gloves, never being 'crossed,' never having anything go wrong in his life, and always having his own way. That is the plain truth and when you realize it, you can control your temper and not before. Until you do realize the truth about yourself, our marriage is off."

Well, believe it or not, he did see the truth about himself. He became honest with himself, and his temper tantrums disappeared.

POINTS TO REMEMBER

1. The salesman's greatest asset is to be believed.

2. Nobody believes a bunk artist. Aristotle once said that about all anybody really gains by lying is not to be believed when he tells the truth. Very few salesmen today deliberately lie to a prospect. What you must watch is the tendency to exaggerate, overplay, or overstate your case. It's better to lose the sale and keep the confidence and respect of your prospect. If you lose a sale, you may reecover it later. If you lose the prospect's confidence, it is gone forever.

3. Your conscience can give you power when it backs you up, but it will choke off your power, when it is against you. Shakespeare said that conscience makes cowards of us all. And so it does, unless your conscience is on your side. Keep your conscience on your side by always being scrupulously honest with prospects, even if it means losing a sale.

4. You can't really be honest with others, unless you are honest with yourself. A person who is dishonest with others tells them lies. A person who is dishonest with himself tells himself "rational-lies." Stop rationalizing your mistakes, faults, failures, and fears and you take the first step toward mastering them.

5. Remember to sell hard, but "sell it right."

8

HOW A SHERIFF TAUGHT ME TO IMPROVE MY MARKSMANSHIP IN SELLING

ONE OF MY BEST INSIGHTS IN POWER SELLING came not from a salesman, but from a county sheriff. C. G. Alexander, former Sheriff of McClelland County, Waco, Texas, was explaining to me how rookies learn to become expert riflemen.

The main thing is not whether you miss or hit on any individual shot. The important thing is to know exactly where the bull's-eye is, and keep correcting your aim.

A man down in the pits behind the targets signals after each shot —showing just where it hit, and just how far the rifleman missed the bull's-eye. After each 'miss,' the rifleman corrects his aim. If the last shot was a 'seven' at three o'clock, the rifleman thinks to himself, 'I was a little too far over to the right. On the next shot I'll have to shoot just a little to the left.'

As long as he keeps the bull's-eye in mind, and he *knows just where his misses are hitting, his misses help him* eventually to hit the bull's-eye.

The Negative Feed-Back Method: Its Application in Selling

Like most salesmen, I had always been afraid of the word "No." Now, it occurred to me that this bug-a-boo might be turned into an asset. After all, if it wasn't for the man in the pits who said, "no," to the rifleman each time he missed, the rifleman would never be able to hit the bull's-eye. Maybe the prospect's "no's" could serve the same purpose for the salesman that the signals from the man in the pits served for the rifleman.

All so-called automatic mechanical devices operate on a principle that physicists call *negative feed-back*. The mechanism is set to *keep going* in the same direction, or in the same way, as long as a positive or "yes" signal is received. But when a negative or "no" signal is received, the mechanism changes its direction or method of operation until it gets back "on the beam."

This is the principle that a self-aiming torpedo employs. As long as a positive signal is received from the target, the rudders do not change. But when a "no" signal is received, then the rudders begin to change the course of the torpedo.

The thermostat that controls the heat in your home operates on the same general principle. If its "target" is to maintain the temperature at 72 degrees, the thermostat keeps right on doing what it is doing as long as the temperature remains at 72 degrees. It is "on target." But the moment the thermostat receives a "no" signal that says to the thermostat "No, the temperature in the room is not 72 degrees," the thermostat begins to *do something different*.

Are your "selling shots" hitting the bull's-eye? It occurred to me that this same principle could be a very valuable aid to a salesman. A salesman is not a mind reader and cannot tell whether his appeals are "hitting home" or not. But with this method, the salesman can stay on the target the same way that a guided missile stays on the target — the same way that the rifleman stays on the target — by making use of "no" responses to correct his aim.

If it doesn't work, drop it! As long as the salesman gets "yes" signals from the prospect, he can be sure that he is on the right track. But when a "no" signal comes in, it means that he must abandon the particular appeal he has been making and try something different.

I began to see that "no" was not a bug-a-boo that I needed to be afraid of. "No" could be a very valuable friend. As we will see in a later chapter, it is well to get a number of "yes" responses from the prospect just before the close to get him in a "yes" frame of mind, but in the beginning of the interview "no" can be used as a very valuable probing action. And, only if you know what the prospect will say "no" to, will you be in a position to know just what will elicit a "yes" response later on.

When I find that a salesman is losing sales because he is afraid to hear the word, "no," I advise him to go out and on the next interview to deliberately try to evoke at least six "no's" from the prospect. He should use these "no's" to correct his aim and then go on to hit the bull's-eye.

The target wasn't there. This principle has enabled me to make many sales that I know would have been lost otherwise. I remember several years ago calling on a man and his wife who appeared to be "in the market" for additional insurance. He was a married man with two children. I used every "family appeal," "security appeal," "pride appeal" that I had. No response.

I pointed out what a fine thing it would be for his wife. I brought out how his children would need their mother at home with them, instead of having her leave them to go to work, as she would have to do if his coverage wasn't adequate. But when I got down to closing, the answer to that appeal was still "no."

I sensed that somehow, I was shooting for a target that wasn't even there. As he walked out to my car with me, I asked him, "Have you ever considered insurance as a personal investment?"

"Well," he said, "I was just wondering if it would be necessary for me to make my wife beneficiary under the policies?"

"No," I said, "You can make your estate or any one else who would have an insurable interest your beneficiary."

"Well," he mused, "I might as well tell you we are on the verge of getting a divorce, and I did not want to get involved in a policy on which my wife would be named as beneficiary at this time. However, I am interested in the policy and if you would write it along the lines you suggested, naming one of my children as beneficiary, then call by my office tomorrow and I will give you the application."

If I had kept on pitching in the same direction in which I had started, I wouldn't have made a sale by doomsday. But by changing my course — in response to a "no" — I ended up writing one of the largest single insurance policies that I ever wrote on an individual.

The Five Targets of a Successful Sale

After analyzing my own sales that had been successful in the past and successful sales of other salesmen I knew, I came to the conclusion that all Sales can be broken down into five basic "targets." A "Sale" is not just one big target — but five little ones, or "five ducks in a row." These are:

1. *Selling the prospect* on looking at your proposition; giving you an appointment.
2. *Selling the prospect* on listening to your pitch in an attentive, open-minded manner.
3. *Selling the prospect* on the notion that he has a legitimate *need* for the product or service (intellectual acceptance).
4. *Selling the prospect* on a *desire* for the product or service; arousing his hunger for your product (emotional acceptance).
5. *Selling the prospect* on the notion that "I want it *Now*" (the Close).

The prospect must be "sold" on each of these separate "small sales" before he will buy the "big sale."

Sometimes you will find prospects who have already sold themselves on the first three "small sales." All that is then necessary is to sell the last two. It is a waste of time and power to attempt to sell a prospect on the first three elements, if he has already "bought" them.

Sometimes a salesman is lucky enough to find a prospect who is already sold on the first four elements — and all that is required is to sell him on No. 5 — the Desire to "have it now."

Occasionally, a salesman will find a prospect who is sold on
Nos. 1, 2, 4, 5, but unsold on No. 3. He may want a new
dictating machine, television set, washing machine, automobile,
but he is undecided on whether he should buy Brand X or
Brand Y.

Sizing up the prospect. An important part of the selling job
is to "evaluate" the prospect in the beginning. Which, if
any, of these "small sales" has he already bought? Then, don't
waste your firepower on targets that have already been hit.

If the prospect has bought none of the five, then he must
be sold on them one at a time and in numerical order. It is
helpful to think of these five elements as steps on a ladder.
Only after the prospect has taken step No. 1 is he in a position
to take step No. 2. Only after he has taken step No. 2 is he
in a position to go on to step No. 3, and so on. Many salesmen
who complain that they cannot "close" would be surprised
to learn that their trouble may not be in lack of power in
the close itself, but simply that they failed to sell the prospect on steps No. 3 or 4.

Only when the prospect has been sold step No. 4 is he able
to reach step No. 5. If you have trouble closing, your trouble
may be that you are trying to take the steps two at a time and
this is simply too big a jump for the prospect. The distance
between steps 4 and 5 is no greater than it is between any
of the other steps.

The "Five-Course-Dinner" Method of Selling

R. P. Brooks, Vice President of National Banker's Life
Insurance Company, refers to these five steps as the "five-
course-dinner method of selling." He says,

Look at these five 'targets' again and you will see that they are
arranged pretty much as a five-course dinner is. First there is the
"invitation" to dinner; getting the prospect to agree to being served
at all. Next comes, not the meat, but the appetizer. You start off
with light food, whet his appetite, make him *want* to eat more substantial fare. You give him a whiff of the steak while it is cooking,
and finally you serve him the heavy fare—the meat and potatoes.
Meantime his mental digestive juices have been stirred into action

and he won't get mental indigestion when your main course is served.

Last, comes the dessert—a pat on the back, a brief bit of reassurance—to leave a *good taste* in his mouth.

Actually, there is a lot in common in the processes whereby a person develops a hunger and desire for food — the way the food is assimilated and digested — and the manner in which a person's mental processes become receptive to ideas and are able to assimilate and digest them. Keeping this analogy in mind can add new power to your selling.

The chapters to follow will tell how I learned, and how you can learn, to serve up each of the five courses in the salesman's dinner, to gain new power in selling.

POINTS TO REMEMBER

1. To make a sale, you must first of all know what you're shooting for, just exactly what constitutes "making a sale."

2. "Making a sale" consists of making five "small sales" or selling the prospect on:
   Looking at your proposition, giving you an appointment.
   Listening to your pitch in an attentive manner.
   Realizing his need for your product (intellectual acceptance).
   Realizing his desire for your product (emotional acceptance).
   Deciding "I want it now" (the Close).

3. The prospect must be sold on each of the five "small sales" before he will buy the big sale. Inability to close is often due to failure to sell one of the preceding "small sales."

4. Keep these targets always in your mind, while selling. Not only will this help you make the "big sale," but even your errors can be put to good account. As long as you know where the target is, and make proper correction for your misses, you can improve your score.

5. Remember that timing is important. Don't try to serve your "main dish" when selling the appointment. Instead, serve an appetizer. Later, when you have the prospect listening to you in an attentive manner, you can serve more substantial fare, topped off by a dessert consisting of a pat on the back to leave a good taste in his mouth after the sale is closed.

9

HOW I LEARNED TO GET MY FOOT IN THE DOOR

In Texas there is an old saying, "the first step in making a rabbit stew is — you go out and catch a rabbit."

Salesmen might well paraphrase it to read, "The first rule in making the sale is to sit yourself down across the table from a prospect."

All your theory and knowledge aren't worth a dime until you get together with a prospect. And unless you can sell the prospect on "opening the door" and inviting you in, you are not going to have a chance to use your salesmanship.

There are two simple ways in which any salesman can add power to his sales. One is simply to go out and knock on more doors. Fred Orr, an investment broker in Austin, Texas, tells me that his sales secret is "Walking, and talking, and telling the truth." If you're not getting in enough doors, you may not be doing enough walking. The other thing you can do is to learn to sell the prospect on letting you in the door after you knock on it.

Sometimes more "walking" is all that is needed.

How Three Salesmen Got Back on Their Feet

I once had three salesmen all in a "slump" at the same time.

They blamed the weather, bad luck, and almost everything else. But I noticed they were spending more and more time sitting around the office piddling. Quite often, all a salesman needs to do to "get back on his feet" is to get *on* his feet and get off the seat of his pants. When I asked these men why they didn't get out earlier, they complained they didn't have any good leads for the morning — all their good leads were appointments for the afternoon.

I suggested that on their way to work in the morning they park their cars at the first place of business on the right-hand side of the street and go in and make a sales pitch. When they had finished, they were to go to the next place of business and continue "door-to-door" until lunch time and the time for their "important appointments."

"Cold turkey" door-to-door selling is not the best way in the world to "get with" a prospect, but it is better than none. I wanted these men to see for themselves that any type of productive effort is better than none.

Their sales began to improve and in a few days there was no more talk of a slump. Another thing happened: They began to develop more and better "leads" so that the need for "cold turkey" selling was less and less.

Jim Perry, Executive Vice President of Union Bankers Insurance Company, recommends "cold turkey" selling for all salesmen from time to time as a sort of "refresher course" or "basic training." He says it keeps a salesman on his toes and conditions him to think on his feet and adjust himself quickly to changing conditions.

"Information without Obligation"

Around the end of the 1940's I noticed, while doing some personal stock-taking, that my records showed I was getting to talk with only about 60 per cent of the people that I tried to make appointments with. If I could increase that percentage, it would mean that much more sales power.

I began seriously looking for ways and means to sell prospects on giving me an appointment. I am not talking about the *mechanics* of developing leads. Most sales organizations have their own systems worked out and the salesman will do best to follow whatever system his own company has provided for him. I am talking about selling your "lead" (your cold prospect) on listening to your pitch, after you have located him.

I began to notice magazine ads because ad writers are some of the best salesmen in the world. What methods did these fellows use on their prospects, whom they could not meet directly, to get them interested enough to write in in response to the ad? If you will examine "coupon ads" in any magazines, you will notice recurrence of certain phrases:

"Please send me your free booklet *without any obligation.*"

"Please send me information about your product *with no obligation on my part.*"

"Please send me your book with the clear understanding that I am under *no obligation* to keep it if I am not entirely satisfied after ten days' trial.

Why prospects won't give you an interview. Most prospects say "no" to an interview for just one reason. It is not that they are really too busy to give you 30 minutes or an hour of their time. It is not that they are not interested in hearing about your proposition. They do not want to *commit* themselves. They do not want to *obligate* themselves. They fear that by giving the salesman the appointment, he may take it as an obligation on their part to buy; and they do not want to commit themselves in any way before seeing the product and learning all about it.

Many times prospects will tell you over the telephone, "I really don't intend to buy right at this time, and I wouldn't want to waste your time."

Instead of arguing with the prospect that he "ought to want to buy at this time" or trying to give a sales talk, I began changing my tactics. I reassured the prospect that it was perfectly all right if he did not buy, that he would be under no obligation to buy, and that I would appreciate an opportunity to discuss with him my product or service *whether he bought or not.*"

This technique increased my own appointments to such an

extent that Jim Perry and I worked out a "foot-in-the-door" technique for our entire organization.

This system, or rather philosophy, for we have no cut and dried "system," increased our percentages of appointment sales to around 90 per cent.

Today the U. S. Army uses this same sales technique in its recruitment program. In order for the Army to get recruits, it must first of all get prospects to the recruiting stations. Many men, however, will stay away even if they are mildly interested in an Army career out of fear that, if they go down, a lot of pressure may be put on them to "join up."

The fear of the prospective recruit is the same as the fear of any prospect. The prospect may half-way want the product. But he is afraid that an effort will be made to sell him against his will and perhaps cause him to do something he really didn't want to do.

So, the Army now has for its recruitment motto: "Information without Obligation." On TV and radio the Army now tells prospective recruits, "Go to your nearest Army information center for 'Information without Obligation.' "

First, You Must Get Your Foot in

Remember the old fable about the camel that wanted to get inside the Arab's tent on a cold night? When the camel asked if he could come inside the tent, the Arab promptly told him "No."

Then the camel changed his strategy. "May I just put my foot in?"

The Arab thought, "Well, after all it wouldn't be too bad to have the camel's foot inside," so he said "yes."

Next, the camel asked permission to put his knee inside the tent. Well, since he already had his foot in, what harm could there be in the knee. So, once again the Arab agreed.

Then, the camel asked to be allowed to put in his leg, his nose, head, shoulders, and so on—one by one—until the Arab agreed to let the entire camel come into the tent.

The crossroads of selling and marriage. I have read where sales theorists recommend attempting to close a sale from the word *go*. According to these theories, the salesman is to approach the prospect with an application blank in one hand and a fountain pen in the other.

His first words to the prospect are, "Mr. Jones I have come to sell you a ———. I am going to ask you to make a decision about this here and now. Please sign here."

Such stories make good reading. But I have never met a successful real life salesman who used them.

They don't use them, because such theories are contrary to every law of psychology and human nature. Prospects have to be "wooed" and "won." They cannot be "forced" to buy, no matter how "dominant" the salesman may be, or how much "personal magnetism" he may have.

You can imagine what would happen if a widow, having made up her mind she is going to sell an eligible bachelor the idea of marrying her, approached him with "Mr. Gotrocks— I want to marry you and I have come to ask you to make a decision about this matter."

The poor fellow would break the door down getting out of there. So would any sales-shy prospect. The widow, however, is too smart to use such tactics. She takes pains to see that the bachelor feels *no obligation*. And, after a time, he may decide that he himself would like the idea of marriage.

Easy Does It

Many salesmen fail to get an appointment, not because they do not have sales power but because their timing is off. They apply their power at the wrong time. Ben Hogan says that the secret of power in a golf swing is knowing just *when* to apply your power. A big muscular marvel can start his swing with enough power to kill a rattlesnake and drive the ball 25 yards, but a 120-pound woman, who knows how to start her swing "easy" and put the power into it at the last minute with a snap of the wrists, can get off a 200-yard drive without too much trouble.

In selling, as in golf, the time to apply full power is not at the beginning but during the last half of the "swing" with an extra "snap" at the very end to close the sale.

Texas steaks are good. Any man is a fool who would not want to eat one. Yet, if you stopped a man on the street, presented him with a two-pound Texas steak, and announced, "I am going to make you eat this *right now*," he would probably run the other way.

Prospects run from salesmen who don't take the trouble to serve an appetizer first, or who try to ram ideas down their throats within the first five minutes of the interview.

Sometimes, the prospect has no appetite at all. He is the fellow who says, "I don't want to buy anything and will not give you an appointment; I don't even want to talk about it."

You must use tidbits at first to arouse his appetite. Then perhaps he'll order your full course.

"Blind Side Selling"

Sometimes it is necessary to approach a prospect from his "blind side." When I was a boy on a farm, we had an old mule that would run like the dickens if he saw you coming toward him with a bridle. But if you walked up behind the mule and hid the bridle behind you until you could place one hand on his head, he would stand perfectly still and docile and allow you to put the bridle on his head and the bit in his teeth. The mule was afraid of the bridle only when he saw the bridle at a distance. If you could once get close enough, he was not afraid of it.

It is strange but true that human beings are also much more afraid of a salesman at a distance than they are close at hand. After he is sitting in their office or on their living-room sofa, he no longer appears to be so fearsome.

Perhaps it is just the instinct of self-preservation asserting itself that makes a prospect automatically afraid of "being sold." Perhaps, the prospects themselves have fallen for the myth that the super-salesman is a sort of Svengali who is able to get people in his "power" and "make" them buy whether they want to or not.

But the fact remains that the resistance to the salesman, or selling, is always highest at the very beginning of the sales interview. The longer he is around the salesman, the less afraid the prospect becomes. Once he more or less "gets used" to the sales interview and sees that his fears are groundless, his defenses let down somewhat.

When you reconnoiter, leave your artillery behind. Larry Breeden, one of our top-producing salesmen, tells me that when making "cold turkey" calls he always leaves his brief case in the car. The brief case is the salesman's "badge" or symbol. It makes him twice as frightening. So Larry leaves the brief case in the car and approaches the door empty-handed and harmless. After he "gets to know" the prospect, he returns to the car and gets his brief case, but by that time he is no longer frightening to the prospect.

Larry McHale, our District Manager in Tucson, Arizona, uses the same psychology when he takes out his fountain pen at the very beginning of the sales pitch. He doodles with the pen, draws graphs with it, and "figures" with it; when it comes time to sign on the dotted line, the prospect is not frightened by the sudden appearance of the fountain pen.

The close really begins in your approach, he says. "If your approach is right, your close will be right and a natural 'follow through.' At the very beginning of the interview when you first introduce yourself, you are in charge. The prospect kicks you the ball when he agrees to the interview. And if you are going to score a touchdown, you must keep the ball and stay in charge of the situation—all the way through—not just at the end.

"No salesmen allowed" Means Easy Selling

R. C. Avrett, our State Manager, in Denver, Colorado, tells me that he is convinced that the reason people put up signs, "Peddlers, Agents, and Salesmen Keep Out" is because of this same vague general fear of the salesman at a distance. "Once you get behind the sign," says Mr. Avrett," you find, not a hard-boiled antisocial creature, but usually a sociable human being. He is usually one of the easiest of all prospects to sell, *if you approach him right*. The chances are that he put up the sign in the first place because he realized that he was an 'easy prospect.' "

People who have an *abnormal* fear of salesmen, have a

reason. The reason may very well be that the person has such a low sales resistance he is afraid he will "buy anything."

Mr. Avrett says that the person who meets the salesman at the door with "I-don't-know-what-you're-selling-but-I-don't-want-any" attitude comes in the same category. Your big hump with such people will not be the close, but the approach.

A four-sentence way to get in the door. I once heard Avrett get inside the door with one of these prospects, as follows:

Prospect: I am not in the market now. I'm definitely not interested in buying anything, and I don't want to listen to any high pressure sales talks.

Avrett: Mr. Blank, I promise I won't try to sell you anything you don't want to buy. All I want to do is *show* you something that I honestly think you would appreciate knowing about. You owe it to yourself to see what I have, and see whether or not you want it.

Prospect: What is so special about your insurance?

Avrett: I'm afraid I can't explain that to you in two minutes, standing out here, but if I could have only 15 minutes of your time, you can decide for yourself.

Prospect: Well, I guess so. Come in. But remember—no high pressure selling.

Avrett: I promise.

(We enter. Avrett begins to "show" the prospect an insurance policy and explain what it offers.)

Prospect: (good naturedly) Whoa, now, wait a minute. You promised no high pressure selling.

Avrett: And I am as good as my word. All I want to do is explain what I have to offer. It is then *entirely up to you* to decide whether you want it or not. I'm not going to try to force you. YOU will be the one to give the verdict, and I'll accept your verdict. But, I am entitled to present all the evidence, in fairness to you, before you decide.

Prospect: O.K.—go ahead.

Thirty minutes later Avrett walked out with a nice sale.

How to "Disarm" the Prospect

In Texas, in the old days, when two men who had reason to

be suspicious of each other wanted to sit down to "talk business," they checked their pistols with the bartender. But the man who wanted to talk had to disarm first.

Salesmen would do well to remember that if you want the prospect disarmed, you must first disarm yourself.

Joseph A. Kennedy, the well-known authority on relaxation, asserts in his little booklet, "Relax and Sell," [1] that prospects who appear hostile and antagonistic are really afraid. They are afraid of the salesman. The prospect sees the salesman as an "enemy."

"If the salesman returns this hostility and antagonism," Mr. Kennedy observed, "the prospect's fears are confirmed and multiplied. Now he is *sure* the salesman is an enemy."

He says that the way to "disarm" yourself is *to relax*. If you get all tense and hostile yourself, you are going to build more tension in the prospect. When men get ready to fight, they get tense. They clench their jaws, ball up their fists, frown, and get set to throw a punch. But when we are around friends we can trust, when we know we are in no danger, then we relax.

"The prospect's subconscious mind knows all this," Mr. Kennedy told me, "and without him realizing *why* he dislikes the salesman, he gets all tense and hostile when he meets a tense salesman who appears tensed for battle."

Salesmen do not carry six guns around on their hips. But they do carry aggressive "fighting" muscles. When you approach the prospect with these muscles tensed, it is the same as if you approached him with your six gun cocked—as far as his subconscious is concerned.

Salesmen have laughed for years about the "low-pressure" salesman who approaches a prospect with "You don't want to buy anything today, do you?" but if you change his pitch around just a little, you can develop a powerful opening to use against a hostile prospect.

When you meet one of those fellows who is all set to slam the door in your face and who greets you with "I don't know what you are selling but I don't want it," remember that he is scared of you. He is afraid of the "big guns" of super sales-

---

[1] *Relax and Sell,* Joseph A. Kennedy (N. Y.: Prentice-Hall, Inc., 1954).

manship that he has heard about. Disarm him by disarming yourself:

"Mr. Jones, I know you do not want to buy anything today and that is perfectly all right. But since I'm here anyway, I would appreciate it if I could tell you about our product so that if you decide to buy in the future, you will know about it."

When the Prospect says, "I'm Not Interested"

Many sales are lost because of the words, "I'm not interested."

A salesman approaches a prospect and says, "Mr. Jones, I'm selling insurance for such and such a company and I would like a few minutes of your time."

"I'm not interested in any insurance," says Mr. Jones, and the sale is lost before it gets started.

"I have some very fine floor mops (defrosters, kitchen knives, or birdseed), Mrs. Smith," says a door-to-door salesman.

"I'm not interested in any mops today," says the housewife and shuts the door in his face."

However, in both cases, it was the salesman's own fault that the interview wasn't sold. The wording of his approach contained an assumption that the prospect might be interested in buying his product or service.

You should never expect a prospect to be "interested" in your product.

Interest must be *aroused*. We become interested in *something* only when we begin to think about it. Right now, are you interested in taking a trip to the South Seas? Probably not. It is the furthest thing from your mind. But suppose you began to look at travel folders. Suppose you read an interesting book about the South Seas. Suppose further that there was a chance you might find buried treasure. You would at least become interested, whether you took the trip or not.

"Prospects are never interested in products or services, as such," Jim Richey, our Regional Director in Charlotte, N.C., tells his salesmen. "Prospects are only interested in those things they have been thinking about. They haven't been thinking about insurance, but they have been thinking about their family, their future, how they are going to put the kids through college, how they can save some money, how they can invest their money to make more. Approach your prospect on the basis of these things that he is already interested in. Then tie-in your insurance to these major interests, *after* you get the interview."

Jim never approaches a prospect with, "Mr. Smith, I'd like to interest you in some insurance."

Instead, he says something like, "Mr. Smith, I'd like to show you an easy way that you can send your boy through college."

Or: "Mr. Jones, I'd like to show you a proposition that has helped many working folks like you and me save some money."

Instead of saying, "I have some very fine mops" (which the housewife really wasn't interested in), the door-to-door salesman might have said,

"Mrs. Smith, I'd like to mop your bathroom floor for you, without any obligation on your part, in order to demonstrate a new scientific principle that cleans and dries with one operation. My company wants to familiarize you with this new principle, which takes all the work out of cleaning floors. We believe if you know about it, you'll eventually buy it; but you're under no obligation to buy from me today."

The housewife, you see, isn't interested in a new mop, as such. But she is interested in getting her bathroom floor cleaned. She is interested about learning something new that takes the work out of a messy job.

Use Friendly Words With Your Prospect

In selling the interview and in the beginning of the interview, while resistance to your being there is still high, use "friendly words."

Sell is a highly emotional word to most people. When they hear it, they get their defensives all lined up. The truth is that no prospect likes to feel that he has been "sold." He likes to think that he has "bought" something rather than that he has been "sold."

Talk, discuss, show, plan, demonstrate are all nonemotional words. Use them instead of "sell" when making your appointments.

"Mr. Jones, I would like about 30 minutes to discuss the welfare of your children." (*Not:* "I want to sell you a set of encyclopedias.")

Mr. Smith, I represent the *XYZ* Company." (*Not:* "I'm a salesman for XYZ.")

My friend Barney Stone, Sr., with the Lone Star Oldsmobile Co., Dallas, never tries to "sell" a prospect an Oldsmobile. Instead, he invites the prospect to "take a look" at the new 98.

When he calls a prospect, he doesn't say, "I'm selling Oldsmobiles, and I want to sell you one."

He says, instead, "Have you seen the new 98? Well, I'd like to pick you up and give you the thrill of driving it yourself, with no obligation on your part."

When the prospect protests that he isn't ready to trade yet and he doesn't want to take up Barney's time, Barney reassures him that it is perfectly all right; he doesn't *have* to buy, but wouldn't he like to go for a ride anyway. Barney then gets the prospect under the wheel and proceeds to let him sell himself. He doesn't try to sell when the prospect is "cold." He waits until the prospect has warmed up to the idea of buying an Oldsmobile by driving it, getting the feel of it; then, at just the right time, Barney "helps" the prospect make up his mind. That way, he says, he doubles his sales power, for he now adds the prospect's selling power to his own.

Prospects Must Be Wooed and Won

Remember that the prospect must be wooed, not forced into buying.

Remember your courting days when you took the new girl out on a date? You didn't try to grab her and kiss her as you were going out the front door. First you got her used to the idea of holding hands, then of having your arm around her shoulders; maybe you didn't even try to kiss her on your first date. You started off with low-pressure selling.

Use the same techniques to woo prospects.

POINTS TO REMEMBER

1. The very first rule for increasing your sales is to "get together" physically with more prospects. The finest sales techniques in the world cannot help you until you are sitting down across the table from a real life prospect.

2. If you're dissatisfied with the number of people you *sold* today, ask yourself how many people you *saw* today. The two go up and down together. The best way to get back "on your feet" during a slump is to get off the seat of your pants and walk toward the nearest prospect.

3. "Information without obligation" is the proper attitude to use when selling an appointment. Prospects hesitate to give an appointment to a salesman because they are afraid they will obligate themselves to buy. Don't try to sell your product when you are selling the appointment. Assure the prospect he won't be obligated in any way.

4. Don't give the prospect an opportunity to say "I'm not interested." Don't try to interest him in your product or service. First sell the appointment. Then, and only then, can you reasonably expect him to become interested in your product. In selling the appointment, appeal to the things he is already interested in: his future, his family, his job, and other personal interests.

5. Disarm the prospect by maintaining a friendly, relaxed attitude yourself.

10

WHAT I'VE LEARNED ABOUT GETTING IDEAS ACROSS TO THE PROSPECT

THE FIRST STEP IN MAKING THE SALE IS TO "get together" with a prospect physically. The second step is to "get together" with the prospect mentally.

You may have the finest pitch in the world, but it is powerless unless it hits home.

Have you ever noticed how radio and TV announcers frequently say, "Please stay tuned to this station; do not turn your dial"? They know that it doesn't matter if they have a million-dollar program being broadcast; it will be powerless unless someone has a receiving set "tuned in" to the station.

I have found it helpful to think of salesmanship as *communication*. The salesman "broadcasts" ideas with his voice. Actually, all any salesman has to "sell" is ideas. If he can sell the prospect his ideas, the prospect himself will then "buy" the product of his own accord. You cannot sell your ideas to the prospect's mind if his mind is closed to your ideas. Neither will he "receive" your ideas if his "set" is tuned to some other station.

Three "call letters" that engage your prospect's attention.
Through the years I have discovered what I like to think of
as "call letters," which alert the prospect to tune in to your
sales talk. A "ham" radio operator first started me thinking
along this line. In order to get a certain friend to listen to
him, he first broadcasts that friend's "call letters." When the
other fellow hears his call letters being broadcast, he immediately begins to listen for the message to follow. He might
have been dozing, reading, or just twisting his dial idly; but
the minute he hears his own call letters, he becomes alert and
listens carefully.

The "call letters" that make a prospect sit up and take notice
and listen carefully are *ego appeal, pride appeal,* and *personal
appeal.*

Talk to the prospect about *your* problems and he listens with
only one ear if at all. He isn't interested in your need to make
a sale to pay your rent. He is interested in paying *his* own
rent. If you talk about your product in impersonal terms,
how good it is generally, and how much it helps people in general; he is only mildly interested. He may even agree with
you intellectually, but his emotions are unmoved. If you talk
in terms of *his* pride, *his* ego, and his personal interests, he
becomes "all ears" and tunes you in.

Someone has said that a man is more interested in a pimple
on his own neck than in an earthquake in China. It is money
in the bank for the salesman to recognize this fact of human
nature.

When you talk about your product in generalities, the prospect hears you but doesn't "listen," like the old time Western
Union operator who heard the steady clakety-clak of the tele-
graph key, but never paid any attention because it was not
directed to him personally. I used to visit in the railroad
station with one of these old-time operators and he would sit
and talk with me and pay no attention at all to what the tele-
graph key was saying. Then all of a sudden he would jump
up out of his chair, grab a pencil, and begin to listen for all he
was worth. Someone was sending a message to *him.*

People are pretty much the same. Always let the prospect

think that your sales message is "for him alone." Remember that women don't take men seriously if they get the idea, "you tell that to *all* the girls." Prospects are human, too, and are flattered if they think your sales message is individual—that you have a "personal interest" in them.

The Importance of Gaining Attention

Dr. Karl S. Bernhardt, in his book *Practical Psychology,* (New York: McGraw-Hill Book Company, Inc., 1953), says, "In order to influence anyone, it is necessary to capture his attention; for the person who can effectively capture and hold the attention of others is the person who can influence their behavior."

I used to think that "attention" was important in selling. I now realize that it is much more than I used to realize. My own experiences and those of our salesmen convince me that getting and holding attention is fully 50 per cent of making the sale.

Not long ago M. J. Harrison, nationally known Insurance attorney and former Insurance Commissioner of Arkansas, and I were discussing this power of attention, and he explained it this way: "Any idea that you give 100 per cent attention to, you will act upon. Ideas are dynamic; that is, they impel us to act. The reason we do not notice this power of ideas more is because there are usually present other ideas that partly inhibit or completely cancel out the power of the main idea. But, the more you can get the other fellow to pay attention to *your* ideas and the more you can take his attention off other distracting ideas, the more you will influence his actions."

In our language we unconsciously admit as much. Armies call soldiers to "attention" before issuing instructions. We commonly say, "He doesn't pay any attention to me," when we mean that he did not follow our suggestions. Of a disobedient child we say he doesn't "mind" us; that is, he does not give us his mind or does not open his mind by paying attention. We seem to realize that if he did "mind" us (give us an open mind) he would "mind" us (obey us).

The "Stop, Look, and Listen" Method

As a handy reminder to myself on how to get and hold attention, I remind myself to "Stop, look, and listen."

The first step in gaining attention is to sell the prospect the idea to "stop" giving his attention to whatever he is attending to when you call upon him. Next you must sell him on taking a "look" at your proposition, on at least "looking it over" whether he wants to buy or not. The third step is to sell him on continuing to "listen" to you with an open, receptive mind.

If possible get the prospect to stop what he is doing and sit still. We can give full attention only when we are still. Try an experiment right now. See if you can hear the clock ticking in your room. Or see if you can hear what the neighbors are saying in the next apartment. Did you become "still," close your eyes, and perhaps even hold your breath? If so, you reacted as most people react when giving rapt attention to something. "He held the audience breathless" is a compliment to a speaker because it means the audience was so anxious to pay attention, they even stopped breathing!

Getting back to the ham radio operator. When he wants to "listen," he first switches off his sending set. When the human mind is set to "receive," the mind is still and the body muscles are passive. So get the prospect away from his "daily routine"; induce his to sit down with you. And don't do or say anything to agitate or upset his mind; remember, to receive, it must remain passive.

How to Make Your Own Connections

If you want to get your ideas across to the prospect and have them well received, you must have some channel for them to travel on. The telephone must have wires to carry its messages. TV and radio have "carrier waves." A salesman, too, must have some sort of "connection" between himself and the prospect, for his ideas to travel over.

Usually when we say "I've got connections," it means that

we have an influential friend who can intercede for us. Having a friend of the prospect introduce you is indeed a good "connection." You are accepted as a friend, rather than an enemy; the prospect "opens" his mind to you and your ideas get across. When you sell one prospect, ask him if you may use his name in contacting some of his friends.

When you call on the friends, introduce yourself by saying, "Your friend Bill Smith suggested that I call on you."

You are no longer a stranger. Right away you have established a "connection" between your mind and the mind of the prospect.

One sale can be a "connection" that can lead to another sale. This is the method that Joel T. Hopp, our State Manager in Nebraska, uses to perfection. When Joel makes a sale, it oftens turns out to be a family affair.

"First, I spend some time trying to break through the 'barrier' and dispel fear and gain confidence," he says. "One of the best ways I've found is to have some close relative "send" me to see the prospect. So when I close a sale, I always ask, 'Don't you have a sister, brother, or some other close relative you would like to have benefit by this same protection?' Any new 'convert' is always anxious to 'convert' others and will usually help you make the sale. Then, when I call on the relative, I begin by saying, 'Your sister purchased a policy from me and she is so well pleased with it she wanted you to look it over too.' "

E. C. Palmer, our Dallas Manager, was telling me recently how he used this same method to sell two $5,000 life contracts with hardly any effort. He had just sold an accident and health policy to a man who had two sons, ages 25 and 26.

When he had closed the sale, he said, "I have something here that your two sons would probably be interested in, for they are young enough so that this plan can make them a lot of money."

The father was immediately interested and arranged a meeting the next day with his two sons. All it required was to explain the plan to them because their father had already "sold them on the idea."

You can multiply your sales if you will remember this one little bit of psychology: a person who has just "bought" an idea feels a compulsion to sell it to others. Ever notice how the man who quits smoking or drinking always starts trying to sell all his friends on quitting?

How a roll-top desk helped me to close a sale. But there are other ways of making your own "connections." You do not need a personal friend. I once used an old roll-top desk as a "connection." I called on a storekeeper who was busy "tending store."

When I introduced myself, he said, "O.K., go ahead and I'll listen while I work."

I knew it was almost useless to attempt to make a sale with the prospect putting up stock and interrupting every two minutes to wait on customers. I looked around for something that I could use for a "carrier" or "connection." In the back of the store, in his private office, I spotted an old-fashioned roll-top desk. I walked to the rear of the store and began to inspect the desk with interest. In a few minutes he walked back to me and said, "I see you're interested in my old desk."

"Yes," I said, "my father had one just like it. I haven't seen one like this for 20 years. I'll bet this old desk has quite a story behind it."

"It sure has," he said and proceeded to tell me the story of the old desk. The desk became a "connection" or "meeting ground" for us. In it we had a common interest and because of the common interest were able to get together. Soon, he was sitting down, letting the clerks wait on the customers up front, and listening attentively to what I was saying. In a total time of some 30 minutes I sold this man, whom I had never seen before, $5,000 worth of stock in one of my companies.

The desk was my connection. But on other occasions I have used clocks, flower gardens, and just about everything else under the sun to serve as a "connection" with the customer's interest.

Get interested in the prospect, and he'll get interested in you. Hobbies make good "connectors." Find out what the prospect's hobby is. If you really know anything about it and can discuss it intelligently, do so. If you don't know anything about it, admit as much; but express interest and ask questions. This is even more flattering. For not only do you have a common meeting ground, but you have ego appeal, for you place the prospect in the superior position by admitting your ignorance and asking him to enlighten you.

The whole secret of making a "connection" is to find some person, object, or idea that the prospect already *knows about* or is *interested in* and tie into that. *Show* interest in what the prospect is interested in. Attention and interest are give-and-take affairs. "As you give, so shall you receive."

First: Show interest and pay attention to what the prospect is interested in. Then, when you get into your sales pitch, you must also show interest in what you are saying if you want the prospect to respond in like manner.

It is not only necessary to "tune in" to the prospect. You must also "turn up the volume" of your own interest, enthusiasm, and will to sell.

Irwin D. Mays, Sr., our Virginia District Manager, once used a bale of hay for a "connection." He called on a farmer named Brown who gave the familiar objection that he already had more insurance than he could carry. He mentioned how much insurance he had on his barns, his cows, his crops, trucks, and so forth. Mays asked how much he had on his own life and found it was only $10,000. He also found that Mrs. Brown was very much interested in her husband having more life insurance.

"It's well that you have so much insurance on your cows and equipment," Mays said, "but don't you think you should be as interested in protecting your wife?" Brown became interested enough to ask questions, but Mays just couldn't close.

"On the way home I analyzed myself to see where I had failed," he said, "and I decided that I had not taken enough time to get close to Mr. Brown. You cannot sell at a distance; you must get close to the prospect. I had learned from Mrs. Brown that his hobby was cows.

"So, the next day I went back out to the farm and found Mr. Brown in the barn. I didn't talk insurance at all, but inquired about his cows. I sat down on a bale of hay; and, as he told me all about his cows, we became quite friendly. Soon we were back talking about insurance, and he listened just as attentively to me. He purchased a $10,000 policy and paid a quarterly premium in advance.

"I will always believe this sale was lost until I took the trouble to show some interest in his hobby. I advise my salesmen to get acquainted with their prospect, show an interest in his personal affairs, talk about his business, talk about his family. Then he will listen to them."

Will D. Darnall, Sr., our District Manager in Alexander, Louisiana, tells how he once made an error and called at the wrong house thinking he had an appointment there.

"Before I knew anything was wrong, I began making my sales pitch. The party became vexed and asked why I was there. On checking I realized I had made a mistake. I immediately closed my case and began talking about bass fishing, about the big one that didn't get away. Well, he was a bass fisherman. After a joke or two, I excused myself and asked his pardon. Some time later this man called me to come to his home and talk about an insurance program, and I came away with a nice check."

Speak the Prospect's Language

If a ham radio operator tunes in a foreign radio station and cannot understand the language, he doesn't waste time paying any attention to it. He dials in some other station. Prospects are pretty much the same. They pay attention to us only as we speak their own language.

"Speaking the prospect's language" can also serve as a tie-in or "connection."

"Here is one of my own kind," he says to himself. "I can believe him and trust him."

Another advantage is the simple truth that we can only understand new ideas in terms of old ideas that we have already accepted. If the new idea seems to "fit in" with the old ideas we have already "bought," it seems logical and reasonable. If it doesn't seem to fit in with our previous experience, we tend to reject it.

I once called on a baseball pitcher and tried to sell him an insurance policy. I wasn't getting to first base until I suddenly realized I wasn't talking this man's language. He didn't "believe in" insurance. Insurance to him was something foreign to his everyday thinking. We never do "believe" in ideas that seem not to fit in to our own experience.

"Well," I said, "do you believe in relief pitchers?"

"Boy! Do I?" he said. "I couldn't get along without them."

"Why do you believe in relief pitchers?" I asked.

"Why, because I just couldn't operate without them. It gives me a good feeling out there on the mound to know that, if anything goes wrong, there's a reliefer in the bull pen who can finish the game for me; that's why."

"Well," I said, "this policy I'm telling you about is *just like* a relief pitcher. It is a lot more important that you finish the game of bringing up your daughter, getting her educated and off to a good start, and making sure that your wife is taken care of. Finishing that game is a lot more important than finishing any game of baseball. A man without insurance is like a pitcher with no reliefers in the bull pen. If anything happens to him, the game will never be finished. No matter how big a lead he may have or how well he is pitching, the game is over when he dies. But with this insurance policy, you can have that same 'good feeling' you spoke about. No matter what happens to you, this policy will be there waiting to take over and finish the game for you to educate your daughter and provide for her and your wife."

"Well," he said, "I sure never thought about it like that." He bought the policy about five minutes later.

The power of "it's just like. . ." I learned something from this sale. The words "It's just like ——" can be magic to a salesman. Since that time I've compared insurance policies to everything from the stock market to a rich uncle. When people reject your ideas, often it's because "they never thought about it like that," as the baseball pitcher said. Your job is to interpret your product or service into terms that the prospect can "think about it" in a way that makes sense *to him*. Just because it makes sense to you doesn't mean it will make sense to him.

The power of identification. Another reason that speaking the prospect's language gets your ideas across is that by doing this you identify yourself with the prospect. You and he become "the same kind of folks," and you yourself are more acceptable to the prospect. I've found that the more the prospect is able to identify himself and his problems with you, the better the chance that he will buy from you. "I'm just a working man myself" . . . "I have to work hard for all I get" . . . "I don't know about you, Mr. Jones, but personally I have a hard time saving money. I say I'm going to do it; but somehow when all the bills get paid up, it just seems to get away. I imagine most folks are in the same boat today." Then go into your pitch about why insurance is the best systematic method of saving.

It often happens that prospects do not object to an idea, so much as to the clothes it wears or the words that are used to express it. If you can learn the prospect's own private language and clothe your ideas in these, he will often accept them. An extreme example of this happened not long ago when Carl O. Edmunds, our District Manager in Salt Lake City, called on a prospect who met him at the door with the statement, "I do not like *agents* — and I don't want to talk to any *agents* — and if I do buy any insurance, I'll get it myself, not from any *agent.*"

Edmunds was alert enough to catch on to the fact that the word "agent" probably had some painful association with the woman and that she would never talk to anyone that she identified as an "agent."

So he said, "Madam, I am not an *agent*. I am the *District Manager* for this company; and when I heard you were interested in insurance, I decided to come out *personally.*"

"Well," she said, "that's different. Come in." And she bought the policy.

Another example of this is the objection that many people

have for the word "substandard." Tell a man with heart-trouble that he is a "substandard risk" and that his premiums will be higher, and he will not buy that at all. Strangely enough, few people will object if you tell them exactly the same thing in other words. For this reason, our companies no longer issue "substandard" risk policies. Instead, we issue "special policies."

Curiosity Holds Your Prospect's Attention

It is as important to *hold* attention as it is to *get* it. One of the best means is by arousing curiosity. The novel that we just can't put down until we've finished it is the novel that arouses our curiosity and keeps us in suspense. Professor Karl Bernhardt says that the unpredictable is what keeps attention.

The salesman who appears to be dead on his feet, who shows no enthusiasm at all for what he is selling, who gives the impression of being half dead and indifferent, is not likely to arouse much curiosity. If he had anything really interesting to bring out later, he would be pretty excited about it himself. The prospect figures he is in for the same old story that he has already heard many times before and loses interest.

I like the story of the old Negro preacher, who, when asked what his secret of holding attention was, said, "Well, first I tells them what I am gwine to tell them — then I tells them — then I tell them I done told them."

The salesman should give some hint of what he is "going to tell them."

The salesman should "promise" the prospect some interesting development to be brought out later on, without disclosing exactly what it is.

In demonstrating a household appliance: "Mrs. Jones, when I get this machine set up, I am going to show you something that you will find hard to believe."

"When I tell you the price, it will surprise you."

"When I get through, you'll say this it the best proposition you ever had."

Mr. J. F. Holly, one of my associates in the real estate development business in Orlando, Florida, provides a very good example of all the principles brought out in this chapter.

When Mr. Holly takes a couple in his car out to see one of the better-located homesites, he usually says something like, "Mr. and Mrs. Smith, a subdivision is like a circus [comparing it to some experience they know about]. In some places there are bleachers, reserve seats, and box seats and I felt you people *would not* be interested in the *bleachers,* but would want one of the box seats [ego appeal]. I have a lot picked out that I believe would just exactly fit your needs [not just a good lot, but a lot for *you personally*]. I just can't describe this lot to you and do it justice, you will just have to wait to see it [curiosity]."

Mr. Holly has found this system highly successful.

POINTS TO REMEMBER

1. The salesman's job is to get certain ideas accepted and acted upon by the prospect. Think of the selling situation as the broadcasting and receiving of a message. The first rule then, is that the prospect must "tune you in." The "call letters" that cause him to pay attention are ideas that have ego appeal, pride appeal, or any other personal appeal.

2. The prospect's mind must be set for "receiving." To achieve this you must arrange for him to be still and stop doing whatever else he is doing. Don't try to sell him while he is actively attending to something else.

3. If you want your ideas to "get across," they must have something to travel on. Make "connections" with the prospect. Find a common interest, bond, or tie-in, where you can have a "meeting of the minds." Hobbies make good connectors.

4. For your message to mean anything to the prospect, you must speak the same language as the prospect. Put your ideas into *his* kind of language. Make your ideas mean something by comparing them to his own experience. Remember the magic words: "It's just like," and use them to translate your ideas into ideas that the prospect already understands.

5. Remember that curiosity and suspense hold attention. Keep the prospect's curiosity alive all through the sales pitch.

11

WHY "I DON'T NEED ANY" IS GOOD NEWS TO THE POWER SALESMAN

THE THIRD STEP IN MAKING THE SALE IS *intellectual acceptance* — selling the prospect the idea that he needs your product. It was a big step forward in my sales career when it finally sank in that it was up to me to sell the prospect on "needing" my product or service, rather than sitting back passively and waiting for the prospect to realize his own needs.

It takes *salesmanship* to cause prospects to realize that they have needs.

Salesmen do not expect prospects to look them up and beat their doors down in order to buy their products. They realize that it is their job to get to the prospect. But many salesmen — and I was once among that number — do not realize that it is also their job to create in the prospect's mind a need for their product.

Vending machine or salesman? The salesman who approaches a prospect with the question, "Do you need any insurance [or can openers or magazines or office buildings]?" is showing the very worst type of passive selling. The prospect's answer is automatically "No." If the prospect *knew* he needed your product, you would be out of a job. He would already have bought it of his own volition.

As C. D. Glaze, President of the Glaze Real Estate Enterprises of Mobile, Alabama, told me recently, "If you wait for the prospect to know that he needs your product, you are no better than a vending machine. You are not entitled to call yourself a salesman."

When the passive salesman hears the prospect say, "I don't need any," he takes it at face value and says, "Well, here is my card. If you ever need any, let me know."

When the active salesman hears "I don't need any," he knows that his job is just beginning. His job is to make the prospect aware of a need he didn't know he had. He realizes that selling the "need" is just as much a sales job as selling the product, and he is no more discouraged to find a prospect who hasn't bought the "need" than he is to find one who hasn't bought the product. The needs that people have and do not recognize are what make salesmanship such a productive field.

When the automobile first came out, very few people realized that they "needed" it. Some time ago, while going through old newspapers in the library, I found an article with a 1904 dateline explaining that the "aeroplane" was just a novelty and would never be anything else, simply because there was no real "need" for such a contraption.

Two X-Rays That Show up Hidden Needs.

Just as a person can have a broken bone or other hidden injury and not know it until the X-ray reveals it to him, the prospect does not know he has a need for your product until you use the X-rays of *imagination* and *demonstration* to show them up.

One of the reasons we find it difficult to see the need of anything that is new to us is that we have no background of experience to judge it against. We simply do not exercise our imagination sufficiently to "see" its possibilities. As late as 1915, when the "aeroplane" was capable of flying hundreds of miles and carrying hundreds of pounds, a lot of intelligent people still couldn't "see" that it was a valuable instrument of war. General Billy Mitchell was criticized and publicly disgraced for saying what any schoolboy of today can "see"; that the airplane could be used to sink naval vessels. Because it had never been done before, had never been "demonstrated," many people said it couldn't be done. And when he failed to sink one particular battleship with one small bomb, the experts said this "proved" that the airplane was not needed at all by the U.S. Navy.

Probably the most common expression heard by an insurance salesman is, "I have too much insurance already; I am insurance-poor." The prospect is sincere; he really thinks he has enough insurance. But the truth is that he has probably never exercised his imagination enough to know just exactly what his needs are in this regard.

How I sold a man who "didn't need any." Not long ago I called upon a young executive. Advanced "qualifying" on my part had established that he had two children, ages eight and ten, had a $15,000 home with an unpaid mortgage, and earned $8,000 per year. When he told me he was "insurance-poor," I said:

"Well, Mr. Jones, you are indeed fortunate. So few men are in a position to know that they can provide for their families in death just as they did alive. Let's see — you have two small children to raise and educate and your wife to take care of. Unless your home is paid for, that will be an expense too. You probably wouldn't want your wife to work, but would prefer that she stay at home with the children. You must have well over $100,000 in insurance."

He looked rather surprised and said that he had $10,000 in insurance.

Now it was my turn to look surprised. I got out my pencil and paper. "Mr. Jones," I said, "I am vitally interested in serving your personal needs, and I would like to ask you a personal question: how much money do you make?"

"I make $8,000 per year," he said.

"Well," I said, "Is that more money than you can spend?

Do you have any trouble figuring out ways and means of spending it?"

"I should say not," he declared. "We couldn't get by on a penny less than I make."

"Well, in that case," I asked "how would your family fare on only $10,000 insurance? It will be 12 years before your youngest child is twenty. At your present salary, your earnings over that period would amount to $96,000. You are going to be worth $96,000 to your family — if you live. If your family needs every penny you make while alive, they will need at least as much if you should die. Your children will soon be in high school, and their expenses are going to increase many times — your girl will need evening gowns and formals, and your boy will need money for dates and dances. Then, too, you are probably thinking of sending one or both of them to college."

Once he began to "see" the actual circumstances, with his imagination he realized his need for additional insurance and purchased a nice policy.

Have you ever noticed that, *before* a person buys a TV set, he always says he doesn't need one? He doesn't like TV anyway, and he wouldn't look at it if he had one. The truth is, he *doesn't* need one, because he doesn't know what he is missing. This is the reason that smart TV salesmen take a set out to the prospect's house and leave it on a free demonstration — without obligation. After the prospect has watched TV regularly for a week or two, he becomes conscious of a new need in his life. By the time the salesman comes to pick up the set, the prospect really "needs" it.

How a hearing-aid salesman creates needs. Another good example is the person who is partially deaf. Usually his deafness came on gradually, and he "got used to it." He invariably says he does not want a hearing aid, and usually gets one only at the urging of friends or relatives who get tired of shouting at him. However, one salesman I know leaves a hearing aid with the prospect for two weeks and gets the prospect to agree to use it during that time. At the end of the two weeks, the prospect has learned just what he has been missing. He now realizes that he "needs" the hearing aid. Demonstration has convinced him of a need he didn't know he had.

Make Your Prospects Dissatisfied with What They've Got

Sometimes it takes only a few minutes to give a demonstration that will convince the prospect he needs your product. If you can get the prospect to "try just for one time" your product or service that is better than the one he has, he often becomes dissatisfied with his "old product" and realizes that he "needs" a new one. This is the reason that magazine ads often have the sales-line, "Send for free home trial." They know that the prospect won't "need" the product until he becomes dissatisfied with his life without it.

Barney Stone tells me that, when automatic transmissions first came out, many people complained that they did not "need" them. "I can shift gears O.K. by hand — it is no trouble to me," they would say. Barney wouldn't argue with them, but would say, "Well, just so you'll know what it's like, let's take a little spin and try it out." By the time the prospect got back, he realized just how much he "needed" the automatic shift, and he was dissatisfied with hand shifting for the first time in his life.

Dr. O. L. Jaggers, pastor and founder of World Church, tells me, "People won't even change themselves for the better until they become dissatisfied with their present way of life and realize there is a better way."

Suppose a tractor salesman had called on a farmer in Abraham Lincoln's time. I can just picture the farmer saying, "Well son, I really got no use for that thing. I'm getting along all right with what I've got — doing as good as anybody else in these parts. Take your contraption to some farmer that needs it."

Farmers were once perfectly satisfied to till the soil with wooden plows and teams of oxen. Now one man with modern equipment can do the work and produce the wealth of 100 or more farmers of olden times. As more and more of his neighbors began using tractors, the American farmer became more and more dissatisfied with his old-fashioned ways. And when he got dissatisfied enough, he went out and got a tractor, too.

"What was good enough for my grandpa is good enough for me — and he got along without any insurance at all," a prospect once told me.

"Well, in that case," I said, "I suppose you light your house with candles. You no doubt have an outside bathroom. Your wife cooks your meals over an open fireplace, cuts your hair, and brings in water from a spring."

I try constantly to make my own salesmen dissatisfied. Otherwise I know they will never progress. If a man is satisfied to live in a small house, drive a second-hand car, and let his wife work to support him, he will never develop the get-up-and-go to have any better way of life.

The salesman who is satisfied to be an ordinary salesman will never make me a good sales manager.

Your Standards Determine Your Needs

An animal has very few needs, because an animal has no standards to maintain. Enough food to keep alive, a mate, and some sort of shelter just about take care of the animal's physical needs. One reason man has risen above the animal world is that man has created standards for himself. These standards, in turn, create new needs that the animals do not have. In addition to purely physical needs, humans have intellectual needs, spiritual needs, and psychological needs.

It is often said that the "American standard of living" is the highest in the world. But it is not so often recognized that one of the big reasons we enjoy better "living" is that we have higher "standards" to live up to. In this country, a bathtub, an automobile, and a telephone are all "necessities." They are "standard" things. In many other countries, they are luxuries. Their "standards" do not require that they have these things — and they don't have them. Until they do make them "standard," they have no real psychological need for them.

Each man writes his own price tag. You yourself have a "standard" that you "live up to" in regard to how much money you should earn, what kind of house you should have, and so on Because of these standards, you think of yourself in terms of a person who earns so much, can "afford to spend so much," and so on. If you begin to think of yourself in terms of a person who should have more and occupy a better place, you'll live up to these new standards. Andrew Carnegie's advice was, "Say to yourself: 'I belong at the top.' "

How to Create Needs by Raising Standards

There are two ways that standards can be used as powerful levers to move the prospect to buy your product. One of these is to sell the prospect the idea that he should raise his current standards.

Before you can sell a man a yacht, you must get him to thinking in terms of a person who "ought to have" a yacht.

"You deserve the best. . ."

"You really owe it to your family and yourself. . ."

"Just about everyone nowadays is. . ."

"You might as well have the best—it won't cost you anymore in the long run. . ."

These are examples of attempting to sell the prospect on raising his standards just a little higher.

By and large, we maintain the same standards as the group with which we associate and with which we identify ourselves. If you can show an individual that members of his own group are raising their standards, it acts as a magnet to raise his own standards:

"Mr. Brown, I noticed so many of your friends are driving Cadillacs now, I just wondered why I hadn't seen you around our showrooms."

"It's reached the point now, Mrs. Smith, where women who keep house and have a family to take care of just about *have* to have a vacuum cleaner [or washing machine, or whatnot]."

We will also raise our standards if we feel they are outmoded or "behind the times":

"These days, washing dishes by hand is virtually a thing of the past."

"I can remember when these automatic typewriters [can openers, juicing machines, gear shifts, or what have you] were considered a novelty, but they've become standard equipment in all modern offices [factories, cars, homes, or wig-wams]."

"Mr. Jones, we used to think that a set of encyclopedias for our children was a luxury item—but now school children almost have to have them to get by."

Remember when the self-starter used to be "extra equipment" on automobiles? Many people thought they didn't "need it." But automobile manufacturers had to make it "standard equipment" when we raised our standards to the point where we felt it was a necessity.

Use the prospect's own ideas and let him sell himself. Probably the most powerful way to use standards in selling, however, is to employ the standards that the prospect *already has* and is striving to maintain. If you can show the prospect that your product will help him maintain some standard, he will see the "need" of your product.

"Mr. Jones, you have a reputation for being satisfied with nothing less than the best—and this product *is* the best."

"Mr. Smith, you are known as a man who does everything humanly possible to make your employees happy—and this product will make them happy."

"Mrs. Brown, folks tell me that you put the welfare of your children above everything else—and this service will benefit your children greatly."

Of course, you can use this technique of spotlighting needs only if you have taken the trouble to learn something about the prospect—what he believes in and what his standards are.

Often, during the interview, however, the prospect will give some clue as to his beliefs and standards if the salesman is alert enough to catch it. If you can "latch on" to some need that the prospect *already* has, then show that your product or service is "just like" it, he can see the need of your product.

I remember once calling on a man who "didn't need" any health and accident insurance because, as he expressed it, "I am forty years old and have never been sick a day in my life."

I could have argued with him—but it is always better to let the prospect argue with himself. I asked if he carried fire insurance on his buildings. He said he had carried insurance on them for 15 years. I asked if he had had a fire in those 15 years, and he said that he hadn't. I then asked him if he was going to drop his fire insurance because this proved that he did not need fire insurance.

"Of course not," he said, "the fact that I haven't had a fire doesn't mean I won't have one tomorrow."

"Well," I said, "does the fact that you haven't been sick or hurt for forty years offer any real guarantee that you won't be in the future? Can you be *sure* that you won't need it in the future, merely because you haven't needed it in the past?"

By demonstrating to him that his need for health and accident insurance was "just like" his need for fire insurance (which he believed in implicitly), I was able to show him his need for my policy, and he purchased it.

POINTS TO REMEMBER

1. When you hear "I don't need it," you are hearing good news. If the prospect already realized his need, you'd be in the same shape as if he had just bought the same product you're selling.

2. Selling the "need" is as much your job as selling the product.

3. Use the twin X-rays—*imagination* and *demonstration*—to disclose hidden needs to the prospect.

4. Needs grow out of standards that the prospect is striving to maintain or standards that he can be induced to acquire.

5. Show the similarity between some "need" the prospect has *already* recognized and the "need" for your product.

12

WHAT I'VE LEARNED ABOUT CREATING DESIRE

THE FOURTH STEP IN MAKING THE SALE IS selling *emotional acceptance*. The prospect must *want* to buy your product or service.

A *need* is an intellectual concept. *Desire* is an emotion. You must sell the *need* to open the door to selling the *desire,* but just because you have convinced the prospect of his need does not necessarily mean he is going to be "moved" to buy your product. We are moved by our emotions. A man can realize a need intellectually and do nothing about it.

A man may know, for example, that he "needs" dental work and do nothing about it until fear or pride or some other emotion creates an intense desire to have it done. A man may know that he needs to quit smoking or drinking or some other habit and do nothing whatsoever about it, until some doctor arouses his emotions by scaring the daylights out of him by "bringing home to him" in a very vivid manner what will happen to him if he does not quit. Elmer Wheeler knew for a long time that he needed to cut down on the food he ate, but he did nothing about it until his emotions were aroused by being referred to the "Fat man's department" in a men's clothing store. He then reduced his weight, and wrote *The Fat Boy's Book.**

---

* New York: Prentice-Hall, Inc., 1950.

It was not a salesman, but Lord Chesterfield, the famous
English writer, who brought home to me the importance of
creating an emotional desire in selling. Here is what Chesterfield wrote that struck home:

Whenever you would persuade or prevail, address yourself to the
passions; it is by them that mankind is to be taken. I bid you strike
at the passions, and if you do, you, too, will prevail. If you can
once engage people's pride, love, pity, ambition (or whichever is
their prevailing passion) on your side, you need not fear what their
reason can do against you.

Another person who helped me understand the power of
desire in selling is Willard Coker, Director of Marshall First
National Bank, and President of Southern Fidelity Life Insurance Co., in Marshall, Texas. Willard has the reputation
of being able to get people to do things he wants done. He is a
good example of President Eisenhower's definition of leader-
ship: "The art of getting somebody else to do something you
want done *because he wants to do it*." Whenever there is a
civic drive, a fund-raising campaign, or any sort of project
where cooperation of others is needed, they always try to get
Willard Coker behind it. One day I buttonholed Willard and
asked him how he managed to get people to do what he wanted
done.

"Pierce," he said, "I can't *make* people do anything. People
fear and resent those who try to force them into doing things.
I never was successful until I learned this lesson. I never try
to make people do things; I only try to find ways to make them
want to. People are not moved by the fact that *you* want them
to do a certain thing, or even necessarily because they 'ought
to.' But if you can find some personal reason for their *wanting
to,* you can count on them to do it."

Bring It Home to the Prospect

Our wants and emotions are aroused by those things that
affect us personally. We read in the paper that 27 people were
killed 2,000 miles away, and we feel little or no emotion. But
if little Jimmy Jones, the kid next door, meets with an acci-

dent, our emotions become involved and we want to do something to help.

In Chapter 5, we saw how selfish wants can motivate the salesman to get out and sell with power. In the same way, selfish wants are what move people to buy your product. This does not mean that everyone you meet is going to be greedy and self-centered. Psychologists tell us that the need to feel important by lending help to others—by "holding up our end of the log"—is one of the strongest wants in human nature. The desire to help others is as much a part of our real self as are the petty selfish desires. Remember that Hugh Roy Cullen, the man who gave away around $160,000,000, says that he did it "because I am a selfish man."

One of my greatest sales. When I founded the Crippled Children's Foundation of America, one of my associates suggested that B. B. Burnett, president of National Foundation Insurance Company, would probably give as much as $5,000. "No," I said, "I believe you are setting your sights too low. I believe he will give a million, if we approach him right and arouse sufficiently his own desire to give."

I knew that Burnett had been seriously wounded in World War II and had been confined in a veterans' hospital for a long time. I knew the pain and misery he suffered, and I knew what it meant to him to be handicapped, having been very active before going in the service. I knew that he was already sympathetic towards anyone who was in the same boat he had been in. I am satisfied that Burnett would have gladly given $5,000 if I had just walked in and asked for it. The desire to give was already there.

Instead, I made several calls on him. I never once told him he "ought" to contribute or that it was his "duty" to give us a donation. My aim was to arouse his own personal "want-to." This was a case of not so much "tuning in" to Burnett's ideas and desires as it was a case of "turning up the volume" of a desire that was already present. On my several visits, I pictured vividly to him the plight of these children. I took him with me and let him see and speak with some of the children. Their needs were "brought home" to him in no uncertain terms. He understood those needs, because his own experience provided a common bond or "connection." The end result of these several visits with him was that he agreed to contribute the entire net profits of his insurance company each year to the foundation. In just a few more years, these donations will total more than one million dollars!

The knack of "making people want to" made him successful. Troy Post, president of the Reinsurance Company of America, is not only an outstanding salesman of life insurance, but has had unusual success in merging two or more big companies. A person unfamiliar with the many problems involved in bringing two or more large companies together into a single organization has no idea of the salesmanship such a transaction involves. There are the egos of the top brass in each company to be considered. There is the problem of bringing two companies—each old, established, and set in their ways—together with a common policy. Yet, Troy has acquired a reputation not only for being able to do this, but for leaving everyone pleased in the bargain. When I asked him his secret, he said this:

"Pierce, there is only one way to do it. You must find good, legitimate reasons why both parties will profit by the transaction. You must then sell these reasons to the two different companies so well that each company has a *personal* reason for the merger. Both parties must feel that *they want* to do it. It is the same principle I have always used in selling insurance. I have always felt that a legitimate sale had profit for *both parties*. The salesman's job is to show the prospect why it will *profit him* to buy."

Troy once merged a young, small insurance company that had alert and aggressive management with an old, established firm that had many times more assets but was at present mainly coasting along on past reputation. The problem was to sell the management of the old, established firm on the idea that it would profit them to merge and turn the reins over to the younger, more aggressive men with the smaller firm. The president of the old firm didn't think too much of the idea.

"Mr. President," Troy said, "when you were younger, you used to drive your own car, and you enjoyed it. Now that you are successful and more mature, you have a chauffeur and you ride back there on the wide comfortable back seat and take it easy. There is no need for you to worry about traffic or anything else. You know where you want to go—you tell your chauffeur—then you leave it up to him to get you there. Now, here's my proposition: In your company here you have a real 'limousine.' Wouldn't it be nice to sit back in the comfortable seat of chairman of the board, and let the president of X company chauffeur for you?"

Troy actually made the fellow *want* to take a back seat— and feel important while doing it.

Make It "Real"

"A person can be told a thing and know it, without realizing it vividly enough so that it affects his behavior," says Dr. G. Colket Caner in his book *It's How You Take It* (New York: Coward-McCann, Inc., 1946).

If the salesman is to affect the behavior of the prospect— that is, get him to sign on the dotted line—he must not only tell the prospect of his need, but must present it so vividly that it becomes "real" to him. The more dramatic you can be in your sales talk, the more you can paint vivid, detailed pictures in the prospect's mind, the more you will arouse his desire to possess your product.

Do not "tell" the prospect. "Picture" to him in detail the pride of ownership, and how your product will make his life happier, easier, or more profitable. Supplement your "picture talk" with diagrams, charts, pictures, doodles, gestures. All these help make the picture more "lifelike."

"Make It Live!"

Lamont Seals, Jr., our district manager in Greenwood, Mississippi, calls this "romancing" and "glamorizing" a sales presentation. "Paint the prospect a detailed picture," he says, "that comes to life. Bring romance and glamour into your picture. These make the picture 'alive,' and prospects are always more interested in 'live' pictures." Seals is also a great believer in the use of the blackboard in training salesmen, for the same reason. "A written word, a graph, a picture, or a chart is more 'real' than the spoken word."

C. P. Brown, Sr., one of our district managers, tells me that he recently had an insurance prospect who seemed immune to all sales pitches until Brown used this "make-it-real" technique. The prospect had a two-year-old daughter. "I pictured to him his home ten years later. His widow and baby are waiting for Daddy's check to buy shoes and school supplies for his little girl. The first of the month comes and there is no salary check from Daddy. This approach was good for $50 per month for ten years." Notice that Brown's picture was *detailed*. He did not talk about "benefits" to the family, or even about food and clothing—he spoke of "shoes" and "school supplies." He did not speak about "lack of money," but pictured the widow and child waiting on the first of the month for a salary check that never came.

R. E. Burns, another of our district managers, is one of our best recruiters of good salesmen. His technique is to find a good man and talk him into "going the rounds" with him. Whether you're interested or not—just ride around with me a few days," he says. He doesn't tell the prospective salesman about the "joy of achievement" or the fun of selling until after he has demonstrated it and let the prospective salesman himself feel it first-hand.

How building a dream castle sold barren lots. In the past nine years, I have had considerable experience selling subdivision lots. I soon learned that I had to dramatize my sales talk. A vacant lot is not too inviting. There is not much beauty in the early development stages of residential property. There are high spots to be leveled off, sidewalks and streets to be put in, barren spots to be covered with trees and shrubbery. One of the best plans for selling lots I have ever found is to take Mr. and Mrs. Prospect to the site and literally "build the house" and "pave the streets" with words.

"Here is where the street will come. Just imagine what a

fine, expensive-looking front yard this will make when levelled off and planted with grass. Your house would probably set right over here. This would be your living room—and here is a nice spot for a patio—and so on."

I learned from experience that salesmen are prone to take too much for granted concerning what the prospect "knows." All prospects know that there will eventually be paved streets in a residential section, that grass will be planted, and so on; why bother to "draw them a picture"? Because unless you do, this "knowledge" on the part of the prospect will not be sufficient to move him.

For example, most people know that insurance companies do pay claims. If you represent a reputable company, the prospect never doubts for a moment that your company pays claims. The prospect "knows" this. But we have found that a very effective manner of arousing desire, especially in health and accident policies, is for the salesman to take a large number of photostats of recent claim payments with him. He spreads these out on a desk top or table and "shows" the prospect some of the recent claims his company has paid.

For the same reason, most real estate dealers today, when selling new homes, arrange to have at least one "show home" or "dream home" completely furnished and ready to live in. A furnished house is more "real" to the prospect than an unfurnished one. I can remember, however, when this was not the general practice. I was once associated with Mr. Bailey Johnson, President of Baily-Johnson, Inc., in Mesquite, Texas. Bailey had a large investment in new houses that were moving so slowly that sales were almost at a standstill. Then we hit upon the idea of having one of the furniture companies in Dallas completely furnish one of these homes. It was a "novel" idea at the time, and we weren't sure whether it was worth the trouble or not. But after making one of these houses "real," Bailey sold a half-million dollars worth of these new houses in 60 days!

Eugene T. Cotton, vice-president of Pinnacle Old Line Insurance Company, says that his sales philosophy is based on the idea that "today" is more real than "tomorrow." Today is here—it is real to the prospect. Tomorrow—or "the future" —is just a vague concept without any form. In selling insurance, we naturally stress the future, but we must picture the future as a "today" in order to make it real to the prospect. We must take him with us into this unknown future, and draw him a picture of a "today" in that future and what that "today" may very well be if he does not act now.

Even this is not always wise, says Eugene. "It is not always well to look into the future with your prospect, for many times he will contemplate things in the future that will leave him in an adverse attitude as to the future protection of his interests. Consider today. You are offering your prospect a plan of saving that exceeds any form of saving or investment. Mr. Prospect today has his earning power, and, in many cases, it is today that he wants to think about, not tomorrow. The plans made today will benefit his interests tomorrow. It is well to consider the prospect's estate today, not 50 years in the future. I suggest that the agent work up a small financial statement with the prospect's help. This will create interest as well as reflecting the value of his present estate. When the assets and liabilities of the individual are calculated, it enables the prospect actually to see the need of more insurance."

Limitations in the Prospect Arouse His Desire

A need in itself does not arouse emotion. If a baby needs a bottle of milk and gets it the minute he needs it, no emotion is aroused. But if he needs it and something interferes with his getting it, then he can become highly emotional. A need plus an obstacle arouses emotion. This is why a crisis can release such power. We may need to take action along certain lines for a long while, and nonetheless drift along until we are met with a crisis that seems to threaten that our goal may be lost forever. Then, our emotions give us an extra shot in the arm— and we are empowered to meet the crisis.

Remember World War II, when thousands of people rushed into stores and purchased things they didn't even need at all, merely because they were "scarce" and the supply was limited?

Dr. Benjamin Spock advises mothers that the way to increase a child's appetite for food is to give the child the idea that the amount of food is limited. Place *small* servings on his plate to suggest a limited amount of food. Once the child gets the idea that there may not be enough food, his desire for food is immediately increased, and he will probably ask for more when he has finished his small portions.

It is common knowledge that many men suddenly get the desire to go out and sow wild oats when they reach the age where they think their time is limited.

Five Magic Phrases to Induce Sales

Mr. C. F. Palm, President of the Great American Health & Life Insurance Company in San Antonio, Texas, has unusual success in selling by direct mail and radio. He uses the power of limitation to arouse desire on the part of his unseen prospects.

"This is a limited offer."

"This offer may be withdrawn without notice."

"To the first 100 people who answer this letter."

"We offer this for the next ten days only."

These and similar phrases have worked for him in arousing desire of prospects that he never sees.

"We have received word that the price on this item is going to be raised within the next few weeks." If this is the truth, it is a powerful arouser of desire.

In selling insurance, we train our agents to find out the prospect's birthday, then tell him, "Mr. Jones, you have only ten more days (or however long it is until his next birthday) to get this policy at the current price. On your next birthday, it will cost you $——— more."

When I made those telephone calls back in 1945, one of my punch lines was, "I am offering this proposition to a small, *select group* of my friends."

Another limitation was the time factor: "There is no time to think it over—the wheels start rolling at 8 o'clock tomorrow morning."

D. C. Bean, our Portsmouth Branch Manager, says that he believes this principle of limitation is the most powerful of all for arousing desire. "The prospect's desire can be created by giving him an example of someone else who wanted my product, but because of his health, he is no longer eligible. I believe most people buy a product mostly when they feel there may be a possibility they cannot have it. This, in most cases, will build a desire to want my product."

Every salesman can use this principle of limitation, no matter what product he is selling. Even if you're selling can openers door-to-door, you can arouse desire by limitation, as follows:

"Mrs. Jones, these can openers cannot be purchased in stores. They are sold only through our own sales representatives."

Or, "Mrs. Jones, this is my last trip through your neighborhood for quite some time. You won't be able to get this product for a long time."

In selling appliances, equipment, automobiles, and other brand products, the principle of limitation can be utilized by pointing out some feature that your product has, that can be obtained on no other product:

"Only our brand carries this special feature."

"No other machine has this."

"We have a patent on this—and you won't be able to get it on any other machine."

Ever notice how advertisements of household appliances, TV sets, stoves, washing machines, dishwashers, even soap powders, pick out *some one feature* of their product and emphasize the fact that this is available *only* on their product?

"The only dishwasher with triggermatic action."

"Only on Myopia TV can you get the new Astigmatic viewing screen".

Ever notice how crowds gather around the counter in a store that has a sign reading: "Only one to a customer," no matter what is being sold?

POINTS TO REMEMBER

1. You can't *make* people buy. You can only make them *want* to buy.

2. People *want* to do things only when they have a very personal reason for wanting to. So don't let your sales talk ramble around; "bring it home" to the prospect.

3. "Make it real" to the prospect. Knowing a fact isn't enough to move a prospect. He must know it vividly and in such detail that it becomes real to him.

4. Use the power of limitation to arouse desire.

13

HOW TO PUT POWER
IN YOUR CLOSE

THE FIFTH STEP IN MAKING THE SALE IS WHAT
is commonly called the *close*. As A. L. Flora, one of our regional directors, says, the close is "selling the prospect the idea *that he wants it today.*"

There is so much misconception about the close that I wish there were some other word to use. Not long ago, for example, a salesman said to me, "Dr. Brooks, I can *sell*, but I cannot *close*." The implication was that *selling* and *closing* were two different things altogether.

In the sense of something separate, standing alone by itself, there simply is no such thing as *the close*. It is *all* selling, right up to the point where the prospect signs his name on the dotted line. And, if you have *sold* all the way, you do not need to worry about that mysterious something called *the close*.

D. C. Bean, our Portsmouth branch manager of Union Bankers Life, says that his close consists of just one sentence: "Do you wish to pay by check or cash?" Everything preceding that sentence has been straight salesmanship.

When the young salesman said to me that he could sell but

could not close, I said to him: "Suppose you and I were at a shooting gallery. Suppose I failed to knock over any ducks, and I turned to you and said, 'I can shoot, but I can't make the ducks fall over'? Suppose I said to you, 'I have good ammunition in my gun; I know how to aim the gun, and I know where to aim it; I have acquired great skill in squeezing the trigger; but, somehow, the bullet just won't knock the ducks over.' If I said that to you, what would you think?"

"Well," he said, "I would certainly think there was something wrong somewhere." He saw the point. Actually, his real fault was that he had not aroused enough desire in the prospect's mind and emotions to make him want the product.

You cannot close a door that has never been opened. And you cannot close a sale that has never been opened.

I have found that if you will forget about the close as something separate and mysterious and instead just think about *selling all the way*, the close is no more to be feared than any other step in the sale.

"I want it now" is the secret of the close. There very definitely is a fifth step to the sale, and it is an important step. You have gotten together with your prospect physically, and have sold the interview; you have gotten together with him mentally and have his attention; you have shown him his need of your product; you have aroused his desire to possess it. Now, all that remains is to *sell* him the idea that *he wants it today*.

Obviously, he cannot want it today, if he hasn't even recognized his need of it. Obviously, he cannot want it today, if his desire for it has not even been aroused. The salesmanship required in the close is getting the prospect to thinking: "Now is the time."

When is the time to close. The time to close is anytime the prospect is ready for it. I have heard it said that the time to close is "when the prospect is ready to buy." But if the prospect is ready to buy, there is no need for a close. The purpose of the close is to get him ready — *now*. The prospect is ready for the close anytime he indicates that he has *some desire* for it. Or, in other words, immediately after you have "sold" the prospect Step No. 4 by arousing his desire. If he has some desire for it, you can work on that desire and shape it into a desire for it *now*.

This may come in five minutes, or after five visits. The salesman must be on the alert to tell when the prospect has "bought" his Step No. 4. But the prospect can't want it *now*, if he doesn't want it at all.

Five Techniques for Changing "I want it" to "I Want it Now"

1. The Piecemeal Close

The piecemeal technique of closing consists in feeding the prospect your proposition piece by piece and getting a "yes" to each piece, until finally the prospect realizes he has bought the entire proposition.

In using the piecemeal close you do not try to get a "yes" to your entire proposition. You take your product or service, select half a dozen or so features, and sell each one of these features separately. It is easier for the prospect to say "yes" to some one feature of your product than to buy the entire product all at once.

For example, an automobile salesman says to a hesitant prospect: "Mrs. Jones, do you like this color?" If she says "yes," she has "bought" the color. Then he says, "Isn't that a beautiful instrument panel?" and her "yes" buys the instrument panel.

Then he says to Mr. Jones, "Mr. Jones — wouldn't it be nice to have that big 200-horsepower motor under your hood?" If Mr. Jones says "yes," he has just "bought" the motor. Finally, after he has covered the entire car, he gets a "yes" to the question, "Don't you believe that is as much car for your money as you could get anywhere?"

After all these "yesses," he gets out his order book and begins to write up the order. If the customer objects that he is not ready to buy, the salesman can then show him that there is really no reason at all why he shouldn't go ahead and get the car now: "Mrs. Jones likes it. She likes the trim and the upholstery. You like the motor and the handling. Both of you like this car, and both of you want this car." He then turns the tables and asks, "Then *why not* go ahead and get it right now?"

Instead of the salesman's telling the prospect *why,* he shifts the burden on the prospect of explaining *why not.* If Jones can't think of any reasons, he says to himself, "Well, after all — why not?" If he can think of reasons he voices them, and the salesman has an opportunity to pin-point his selling on these points.

The piecemeal close is psychologically sound. We can digest an idea easier a little bit at a time, just as we can digest our food better if we take it bite by bite instead of trying to swallow it whole. Sometimes the prospect just cannot bring himself to accept the idea of his buying your product, if it is put up to him all at once; he has to get used to the idea, a little at a time.

The beauty of the piecemeal close is that, after the prospect has "bought" each separate part or feature of your proposition, there really is no reason why he should not "have it now." In his own mind, he has already "bought" your product. Once he realizes this, he sees that he might as well go ahead and take delivery.

Remember, the word *buy* is often used as a synonym for *agree* or *accept.* "Let's go to Joe's steak house," a friend says. "I'll buy that," you say — meaning that you have accepted his idea and agree to the proposition. Once the prospect "agrees with" or "accepts" your product in his own mind, he has, for all practical purposes, already "bought" it.

One "yes" leads to another. Another reason the piecemeal close is so effective is that, once a prospect has said "yes" to one feature of your proposition, it is much, much easier for him to say "yes" to another feature. Dr. Harry Overstreet has said the reason for this is that, after we mentally give assent a number of times by saying "yes," we get into a "yes" frame of mind. If you have gotten a half dozen minor "yesses," you have literally *conditioned* the prospect, so that, when you come to the $64 question, he finds it much easier to say "yes" in his own mind.

2.   The Implied-Consent Close

After you have "sold" the prospect on some of the separate features of your product, it is well to *assume* that he has already bought the entire proposition, and act on that assumption.

"Mr. Blank, you would like your wife to have the protection this policy offers, wouldn't you?" (Yes)

"You also like the savings feature?" (Yes, I do)

At this point, get out the application form, begin to fill it out, and ask whether he would rather pay on a quarterly or an annual basis.

Implied consent closes million stock sales. Don J. Willmon, President of United Bankers Life Insurance Company, Dallas, Texas, tells me that he believes more sales are lost over this one thing than any other: The salesman does not accept the fact *in his own mind* that the sale is closed. He keeps on talking and talks himself out of the sale. If he would assume, at the proper time, that the sale is closed, the prospect would follow suit.

"I base my reasoning upon one experience which I have had personally, and with which you are already familiar," he said. "In capitalizing a new company, I sold over one million dollars worth of stock in 30 days, relying solely on the fact that all my prospects had implied their intentions of buying the stock."

It is well to realize that there is a psychological moment when the prospect isn't quite sure himself whether he has bought or not. In changing from the idea of "I don't see any need to buy" at the beginning of the interview to "I want this now" at the end of the interview, the prospect's mind literally "turns over" from "not-buy" to "buy."

William James compared changing our belief from one idea to its opposite to turning a cube over, so that, instead of resting on one base, it "flops over" on another side. At the midway point, the cube is delicately balanced and could easily fall either way. At this point, the salesman's assumption that "you have bought" is all that is necessary to convince the prospect. But if the salesman misses the cue, the prospect thinks to himself, "I guess I haven't bought that, because the salesman is still trying to sell me."

G. L. Meyers, one of our top-notch producers, says, "In closing a sale, I never ask a prospect if he wants to buy my product, but *when I think* he is sold I start writing up the application. I start asking him about his health, height, weight, and so forth. I always ask him for his full name last. When the application is completed, I hand the application and my pen to the prospect and ask him to give me his O.K. by his signature. This usually works, but if he stops me before I get this far along, I merely do some more selling then go ahead with the next question to be answered on the application."

W. W. Cordes, of Houston, Texas, one of the best salesmen I've ever met, says, "In closing, I usually take the initiative and assume that what they want to do is take advantage of this opportunity. Depending upon the client, I might hand him a questionnaire of physical ailments and ask him to read it and see whether or not he could qualify, or I might ask for several references of people who could recommend him."

Implied consent is one of the most powerful techniques in selling. If it is done correctly, some rather amazing and almost unbelievable results can sometimes be obtained.

I have heard Charles G. Eidson, President of American Bankers Insurance Company of North Carolina, tell how he once sold a ticket agent an insurance policy while waiting in a railroad station to catch a train. Time was short, and, more or less on a lark, Eidson decided to see whether he could make a sale. He walked up to the window, pulled an application blank from his pocket, placed it on the counter between them. He introduced himself and began immediately to explain his proposition, filling out the application blank as he went along. He continued right on down to the bottom where there was a receipt attached. He filled out the receipt, tore it off, and handed it to the ticket agent, and at the same time said, "Sign here, please." The agent signed the application, took the receipt, and handed Charley a cash payment — without ever saying a word!

3. The No Decision Close

Sometimes you can sense that the prospect likes your proposition and is interested, but, if he is pinned down to making a definite decision, he will probably reject it. These are the prospects who "just can't make up their minds." By using the "no-decision close," it is possible to close the sale without the prospect ever making a definite final decision.

Many department stores make use of this technique. They have found that a policy of "If you don't like it, bring it back" will sell many times more goods.

A woman comes into the store and sees a hat she likes. She plays with the idea of buying it, but isn't quite sure. Maybe she won't like it when she gets it home. Maybe her husband won't like it. If she is forced to make a decision right there at the counter, she may not buy at all. But the clerk says to her, "Madam, don't try to make up your mind now. Take *two* hats home with you. Think it over at home and decide. If you don't want them, bring them both back." In about 90 per cent of the cases, she takes both hats home and keeps both of them, for to return one of them would again require her to make a decision that she dreads.

I used this technique when I made those telephone calls back in 1945. When I reached the point where the other person said, "Well — er — I just don't know. I'd like time to think it over. This is a big order on short notice," I'd say, "I don't want your check tonight. All I want is your *nod*." Thirty-four of them gave me their *"nod"* and later mailed their checks.

"Just try it for ten days at our expense — then decide" is a favorite phrase of direct-mail advertising, and a powerful one, because it relieves the prospect of making an immediate decision.

Many times, I used to say to a prospect who was hemming and hawing — "Well — let's just fill out this form for your medical examination now, and if you decide you don't want it tomorrow, there's no harm done."

You can turn the tables on those people who can never make up their minds by making their power of indicision work *for* you instead of *against* you. Simply place them in a position where, in order *not* to buy it, they will have to make a decision. Many book clubs use this technique. They realize if they have to wait for the member to make the decision to send in *for* a book, they may lose a sale. So, they send a card each month for the member to return if he *doesn't* want the book; otherwise, it will be sent to him.

Travis Wallace, President of Great American Reserve Insurance Company, one of the nation's outstanding sales executives, is a master at using the no-decision close, which he uses in conjunction with the implied-consent close. His close is so smooth that the prospect himself doesn't realize just when he decided to buy. It has been said that "Trav" is a master at "letting" the prospect buy.

R. E. Dowdy, our District Manager at Memphis, recently got a lead on a woman who was in the market for accident and health insurance. She was already sold on everything except which policy she should buy. When Dowdy called on her, she said, "Just leave these folders and prices with me, and I will make up my mind."

"Mrs. *X*," he said "I'll be glad to leave you these folders, but I'd like to leave you something much more valuable — a receipt showing you are insured."

"I never do anything on the spur of the moment," she demurred. "I want to look around."

"Well, Mrs. *X*," Dowdy said, "you are going on your vacation in two weeks [*limitation of time*], and you should have this coverage. I appreciate you want to get the most for your money [*agreement*], but the only way you can possibly be sure you buy the best policy is for you to know in advance what you are going to the hospital for. In that event, you might check around with the several hundred different companies that write this type of coverage and buy the best for any one particular type of sickness, but of course if you were already sick it would be too late to buy hospitalization with any company.

"I am in a position to do something for you *today* that will be very important to you. If you will submit your application *today*, this policy will be in force in just a few days for all accidents and most sickness. And, although I expect you to keep looking around to see what other companies have, at least you will have the peace of mind in knowing you have some protection in force. This will be worth a lot to you, since you're going on your vacation. Now, I'm going to suggest that you pay the premium on either an annual or semiannual basis to start with, and *then you can decide later* how you want to handle it *regularly*."

She bought the policy.

4. The "You've got nothing to lose" Close

Psychologists have found that we buy with our emotions. First, we want something, then we think up "reasons" to justify what we want.

A woman sees an expensive hat that she feels she cannot afford to buy. But she wants the hat badly. She begins to look for "reasons." "Oh, well," she says, "you might as well get *some* enjoyment out of life," or, "If I'm dressed up it may help John get that important contract."

The "you've-got-nothing-to-lose" close furnishes the prospect with a reason or excuse for going ahead and doing what he really wants to do.

In selling houses, I frequently say to a prospect, "Well, you're paying for somebody's house *now;* it might as well be yours as your landlord's."

In selling insurance, I frequently point out that you cannot lose — it really doesn't "cost" you anything: either you or your widow will get back every penny you put into it, plus free protection for 20 or 30 years.

Johns Manville salesmen say, "You're paying for this insulation now in your heating bills. We guarantee you will save enough on your heating bills to pay for the insulation. Since you're paying for it already, why not have it?"

C. F. Bennett, our District Manager in Wilson, N.C., says that many times, when prospects object to price, they are really hoping you can convince them and are looking for some rationalization so that they can feel comfortable about spending the money. When a prospect says the annual premium is too high, Bennett says, "Well, Mr. Brown — after all, that isn't very much money if you consider that it is only $46.10 quarterly. Where else can you buy peace of mind for fifty cents a day?"

5.   The "Make them say 'No' " Close

I used to try to avoid a "no" at all costs. Then I discovered one day that prospects were as afraid of "no" as I was. When I discovered this, I made it a rule to never give up on a sale until I had received at least one, and usually six, definite "no's." I never use this technique until all else has failed. But before calling it quits, I must hear a definite and clear-cut "no." When I began using this technique on so-called "lost sales," my percentages of closings went up surprisingly.

"No" is the hardest word in the English language to say. Prospects dread saying it almost as much as salesmen dread hearing it. Don't you find youself doing many things — serving on committees, accepting invitations — simply because you can't say "no."

Using the "crisis close." At the very beginning of the interview, it is fairly easy for the prospect to say "no." He is under no obligation, psychological or otherwise, to you. He may not even know you, and never have seen you before. Subconsciously, if not consciously, he knows that, if he gives you the interview and listens to you, it is going to be difficult for him to say "no." That is the reason he attempts to brush you off on giving you the interview. Also, for this reason, the more sales resistance a person shows in giving you the interview, the easier he is likely to be to close.

At the end of the interview it is a difficult thing for the prospect to give you an unqualified "no." Many salesmen may not believe this. If you are one of them, ask yourself, "Did my prospects really say the word 'no,' or did they use some evasive sentence such as 'I'd like to think it over' — 'I don't think so' — 'I'm going to look around first' — 'not today' — 'I can't afford it' "?

These are all evasive answers that the prospect uses to get off the hook to keep from having to say "no." If you pick up your hat and leave when you hear one of these evasive answers, you haven't made the prospect say "no." Making him say "no" might be called the *crisis close.*

Remember the power of crisis that we talked about in Chapter 2? Remember that a frog will not jump out of lukewarm water? Customers will not jump at lukewarm closes. Make the water hot for them, and they will jump. Pin him right down to a yes-or-no proposition. Put the prospect on the spot where he either has to say "yes" or "no."

One way to do this is to say something like: "Mr. *X*, I am going to ask you to make *a definite decision* in this matter that is of tremendous importance to you. If you say 'yes,' it means that you can have the security and peace of mind of knowing that your loved ones will be taken care of — you will be saving for the future — [and other strong points of your proposition]. On the other hand, if you say 'no,' it means that the future of your wife and children is insecure [and so on]. Now, Mr. *X* — is it going to be 'yes' or 'no'?

In using this technique, no matter what you're selling, always paint the prospect a vivid picture of what it means to him if he says "yes" and what it means if he says "no." Since you are using this technique only as a last resort, you have nothing to lose. Prospects will not resent a strong and definite close.

"I have found it important to remember that buyers like strong closers," says W. B. Adams, our Charlotte District Manager. "A person who commits himself to an appointment with a salesman becomes a prospect and he does not expect to be coddled by a friendly visit. He expects the salesman to try to make the sale and therefore, unconsciously or intentionally, he makes the job of the salesman a difficult one. He wants and expects the salesman to be a strong salesman. Nothing is more disgusting to a prospect than a meek and lifeless agent or salesman."

Prospects, it seems, do not like to be "easy marks." They like to make the salesman earn his pay — therefore, they like strong closers.

Howard S. Wright told me not long ago how he had just

used the "make-them-say-no" close. The wife wanted the hospitalization plan. The husband agreed they needed one, but he kept finding reasons for delaying. First, he wanted his lawyer to read the contract. Next, he wanted it to study at home a few days. When Howard was almost ready to give up, he handed the prospect the application and pencil and said as a last resort, "Mr. Blank, I would like you to make a definite decision now as to whether you want this or not. Tell me either yes or no." The prospect signed the application without another word.

Of course, you will lose some of these "crisis" closes, but you would have lost them anyway if you hadn't tried, so why not try it when all else fails?

POINTS TO REMEMBER

The "close" is no mysterious something that is added on at the end of your selling pitch. It's **all** selling—all the way. If you have sold an intellectual need for your product and aroused an emotional desire for it, all that remains is to sell the idea, "I want it **now**." Use these five techniques for selling "I want it now":

1. *The Piecemeal Close.* You sell the prospect your product or service a little bit at a time. Sell each small feature separately, then merely remind him that he has already *decided* that he wants each separate feature; therefore, he might as well have the whole thing now.

2. *The Implied-Consent Close.* The prospect has indicated he wants it, so you *assume* that he *must* want it now and *act on that assumption.* This is a powerful close that often works wonders. Its advantages are that it sidesteps lots of arguments and fictitious objections. You don't *ask* the prospect if he wants it now—you simply act as if it were a foregone conclusion that he does.

3. *The No-Decision Close.* This allows the prospect to "have" the product without ever having to face making a definite, irrevocable decision. It often works wonders on those people who find it very difficult, if not impossible, really to make up their minds to anything definite. When you use this close, you arrange things so that the prospect will have to face making a decision *only if he decides he doesn't want it.* "If you *don't* want the book selection for this month, mail in the card." "If you decide later you *don't want* this policy,

there is no harm done." "Take these hats home with you and think about them. If you decide that you don't want them, bring them back and we'll gladly refund your money."

4. The "You've-Got-Nothing-to-Lose" Close. This furnishes the prospect with a logical "reason" that he can justify to himself, the fact that he does want it. "You might as well get some pleasure out of life." "You're paying for this service already—why not have it?" "You shouldn't regard this as an expense, but as an investment."

5. The "Make-Them-Say-No" Close. To be used only as a last resort. Don't accept an implied "no." Refuse to take an evasive answer. Pin the prospect down and make him give you a definite, unqualified "NO." Since prospects dread saying the word "no" almost as much as salesmen dread hearing it, you can recover many lost sales by refusing to take "I guess not" and such evasive answers as synonyms for "no."

14

HOW TO INSURE YOURSELF AGAINST FAILURE

THOUGH FEW SALESMEN WILL ADMIT IT, FEAR often robs them of more than 50 per cent of their potential power: fear of "big shots"; timidity about "approaching" people; and, after the approach has been made and all is going smoothly, fear that they won't be able to close.

I know from personal experience that *fear* alone has robbed me of many sales.

Turning from "passive" to "active" will go a long way towards relieving any salesman of his anxiety and nerves. Anxiety and fear thrive on inaction. It is the period *just before the battle* when soldiers feel the most fear. It is while you are passively idle, speculating about the outcome, that fear grips your soul. Once you are organized for *action toward a positive goal* and commit yourself 100 per cent toward achieving this *one goal,* and "get into action," it is surprising how your jitters subside.

The idea that did most to rout fear from my own selling was a casual remark made by an old friend of mine, a man eminently successful in the insurance field.

This Idea "Insures" Your Own Success

A group of salesmen were indulging in the salesman's favorite indoor sport: relating their experiences — telling of the "big ones that got away" and the big ones that had been landed. One salesman was telling of a prospect he was to call on the next day with possibilities of a $100,000 policy. "Boy, I sure hope I don't lose that sale," he said.

Bert A. Hedges spoke up: "Just remember, young fellow, you can't 'lose' a sale you never had. You've got nothing to lose, because you haven't got the sale tonight — and if you don't get it tomorrow, you won't be any worse off than you are tonight."

The young salesman seemed to relax. His relief was visible and you knew that he would approach his prospect in the morning with more self-confidence and more power. But then an idea occurred to him.

"That's fine, Mr. Hedges, but what happens if I adopt that attitude about *every* prospect, and none of them buy."

"Son," said Bert Hedges, "insurance companies deal in 'averages.' You don't have to worry about individual prospects. All you have to worry about is making enough calls."

The Individual Is Unpredictable

Well, all this was certainly nothing new to me. I had heard and even preached the value of getting out and making calls — of putting your trust in the "law of averages."

I remember, when I was with Real Silk Hosiery years before, we had a sales manager who used to say, "The law of averages will take care of you — if you'll only get out and make enough calls. You don't even have to be a good salesman if you're willing to make enough calls. The object of learning salesmanship isn't to enable you to sell — anybody can do that — but rather to enable you to improve your batting average."

I had read that "the individual is unpredictable, but man in the mass is a mathematical certainty." But, although I derived benefit from these teachings, they never seemed to "sink in" or "hit home" as they did when Bert Hedges said, "Remember, son, insurance companies deal in averages." Something rang a bell in my own mind. I saw this business of "making calls" in a new light, and I saw for the first time in my life how "uncertainty" in selling could be removed. I saw how a salesman could literally "underwrite his own success" and take out his own insurance against failure.

If you analyze it, most fear in selling comes from the basic truth that, when pin-pointed to any one individual sale, selling is the most unpredictable, most uncertain, most insecure profession in the world. There is no system ever yet devised that can *guarantee* that *any individual sale* will be successful.

We cannot lick fear by dodging issues, so let's face it: an individual sale is *uncertain.* There is no way on earth to know whether you are going to sell or not. This book cannot tell you how. No one on earth can tell you how. While we're facing facts, let's go whole hog: There is no way on earth you can tell when you start out in the morning whether *that particular day* is going to be productive or not. The individual is unpredictable, and the best salesmen in the world miss individual sales.

But man in the mass is a mathematical certainty. Happily for the salesman, the foregoing is only one side of the picture. The salesman who sees only that side of the picture is like the man who cannot see the woods for the individual trees.

Had you ever thought about the fact that insurance companies take even a bigger gamble than the salesman? Can you imagine anything more uncertain — more risky — than trying to predict exactly how many years any one individual person will live on this earth? Take one of your friends. How would you like your success or failure to depend upon whether or not you could guess to the very year how long he will live?

Your first step would probably be to get a doctor to examine Bill and give you a report on his state of health. Yet how many doctors do you know who have the ability to tell exactly how long any individual person will live? You'd probably want to know something of Bill's heredity. Here again, you'd just be guessing — but you would have a few known facts about Bill to base your guesses on.

But, now let's suppose that your success or failure depended upon your ability to guess whether or not Bill would have an accident? You could study Bill from now to Kingdom come — you could trace his family tree back to Adam — and you would have absolutely no way of knowing whether Bill is going to have an accident or not. The very word "accident" implies an unplanned, unpredicted, uncertain, unexpected something.

"No business on earth," you say, "is as insecure, as un certain, as the insurance business."

But let's look at the facts. Which are the most stable businesses in our country? Which businesses keep going through good times and bad? Which businesses offer the most *security* to an investor? Go to any business analyst, go to your own stock broker, and tell him that you have money to invest, but that you want an absolutely *sure thing* — that you want to put your money where you can be sure it is *absolutely safe,* where you can have a *guaranteed dividend.* He will tell you, "Invest in insurance." It is so safe — so sure — so certain — that even our banks invest their money in insurance for a "guaranteed return."

What's the Secret?

How does it happen that this most uncertain of all businesses is, at the same time, the most stable in the country?

Insurance companies guess wrong on many, many individual policies. The truth of the matter is, they *can't* tell you how long Bill Jones will live, anymore than you can tell whether or not you'll be able to sell Bill your product or service. But they also know that if they have enough Bill Joneses, the averages will remain stable and predictable. The more policy-holders a firm has, the more stable its business becomes. They do not depend upon individuals, but upon *averages.*

Spread the Risk

An insurance company takes a tremendous risk on Bill Jones the individual. But do insurance executives sit up nights worrying about whether or not they have guessed wrong on

Bill? Do they worry themselves into ulcers if they pay out $50,000 on Bill after he has paid only one monthly premium?

They do not give the *risk* they are taking on Bill Jones a second thought, because they *spread this risk* over thousands of policyholders. They know the law of averages will take care of them. Instead of worrying about it, they are most anxious to *take more risks* by insuring more Bill Joneses — the more the better. Insurance companies do not *have to* make a profit on Bill Jones.

It's "Guaranteed"

In just the same way the salesman can turn one of the most uncertain occupations into the most stable in the world if he will follow the example of insurance companies and *spread the risk*. If he will get out and make calls, and make enough of them, the law of averages will begin to "insure" his success. Toss a coin *one time* and it is the most uncertain thing in the world as to whether it will come up heads or tails. Tell me that you intend to toss it 10,000 times, and I can predict that it will come up 50 per cent heads and 50 per cent tails.

With no selling ability whatsoever, but depending purely upon chance, your chances are 50-50 that you can be successful as a salesman — *if* you'll get out and make enough calls.

"I've Got Nothing to Lose"

The salesman who sits down and "wonders" if he is going to be successful on any individual call is passive. He is thinking about failure at the same time he is hoping for success. Within a matter of minutes, it is possible to work yourself up into such a state of anxiety that, by the time you call on your prospect, you have practically insured your own failure by letting your fear rob you of self-confidence. You go into the interview in a *negative* frame of mind and with your *power cut off*. You cannot *turn on the power* when you are anxious, fearful, tense, and afraid. You become so anxious to make a good impression that you make a bad impression.

A cure for pre-sale jitters. I have found that the only cure for these pre-sale jitters is to go back to the law of averages. Don't "wonder" about the individual sale. Don't give whether you will succeed or fail any thought. Remember that one individual sale is neither going to make or break you.

Be perfectly willing to fail on any one individual sale, and it is surprising and dramatic how quickly your fear of not making the sale leaves you. Have a little talk with yourself and thoroughly understand that you are going to miss some sales. It's all a part of the game. Get used to the idea of missing a few.

"Get Used" To Missing

Tom High, Agency Director, Union Bankers Life, has a theory that you need to train a new salesman to "get used" to failure, so that he will not be so terribly afraid of it. Many sales managers, when they are working with a new man line up a series of "pushovers." The idea is to convince the new salesman what a breeze this business of selling is — and what a great salesman his manager is. Not Tom.

"I always manage to miss a few," he says. "I want my salesmen to get over their unholy fear of failure." Tom goes out with the new salesman; he sells a few, and he misses a few. When he misses, he never complains or appears discouraged. If the new salesman comments about a "miss," Tom just passes it off as if it were a matter of no concern: "Oh, all of us miss a few, but the beautiful part of this business is that *you don't have to make a sale* on any individual customer."

The new salesman goes home that night and says to himself, "Well, after all, Tom High misses sales and it doesn't seem to worry him — and he certainly seems to be doing all right." His *big fear* about his job — that he won't be able to sell — is partly overcome. Later, when he goes out on his own and misses one, he will not be completely overwhelmed, discouraged, and down in the dumps.

I was talking to Bert A. Hedges a few months before his death, and he said, "Pierce, the proper mental attitude before calling on a prospect is, *'I've got nothing to lose.'* Remember, you can't lose a sale you've never had."

Yash Young, after the age of forty, took up selling for the first time and became one of the most successful insurance salesmen this country has ever produced. He said that he made it an iron-clad rule that he would absolutely refuse to go into any proposition if the outcome had the least power to disturb him in any way. He would decide ahead of time, before making the call, that failure to sell this deal would not disturb him, or he would not make the call at all.

Sam Keith, one of our oldest producers, carries this philosophy a little further. Once having decided that he is not going to call on the prospect at all if the outcome is going to disturb him, he says to himself: "Since I'm not going to call on him at all, I've already *lost that sale*. It will remain a lost sale as long as I do *not* call on him. So, I now have nothing to lose by going ahead and calling on him."

Childish? You wouldn't think so if you took a look at his production records. You would then decide that it was a smart bit of "self-salesmanship" for relieving the presale jitters and getting oneself in the proper frame of mind to make a sale.

Be Willing to Strike out

When I say, "Be willing to miss a sale and you will find yourself suddenly with a new power to make the sale," it may sound contradictory. But it will seem so only if you are again looking at the individual trees instead of the woods — only if you feel that your success or failure as a salesman hangs on one individual sale.

Look at the salesmen you know who are poised and sure of themselves — who do not become overawed before calling on a "big prospect"; who apparently don't care too much; who are not overanxious to make the sale. What is their poise and confidence based upon? Is it that they have no ambition — that it really "doesn't matter" — that they do not want to sell?

No; it is based upon something much deeper. It is based upon a *supreme confidence* in salesmanship itself — and in their ability to sell successfully *in the long run*. They are so *sure* that the law of averages will pay off — so *confident* that

they can end up the season with a good batting average —
that they can afford to "strike out" occasionally. They know
that if they keep going to bat, they are going to have their
share of strike-outs. They also know that if they never go to
bat at all — if they never go up there and get their quota of
strikeouts — they are never going to get a hit.

They *want to sell* the individual prospect. They try their
best to sell him. But they are not overcome with fear, because
it is not a life-or-death matter. Unless you're willing to get
up there and take your cuts — knowing that you are going
to strike out occasionally, you are never going to get to first
base in the selling game.

This Releases Power

Place a man in a situation where he is convinced that the
outcome is going to be failure, and his will to act becomes
paralyzed. Place a man in a position where the outcome is in
doubt, and his will to act is seriously crippled.

Salesmen who "piddle" — who find excuses to hang around
the office, who have difficulty "getting started" — are not
basically lazy, but *afraid*.

When the outcome is in doubt, it is easy to be passive and
not act at all. It is easy to think up excuses to convince yourself why you shouldn't get out and beat the bushes.

But suppose your success was "insured." Suppose it was
"guaranteed." Suppose someone came by your desk and said,
"Bill, I know a prospect who is all ready to sign up. I can
guarantee if you go over to his office, he will give you a $100,000
policy."

There wouldn't be enough men in the office to hold you.
You wouldn't have time to stop for a cup of coffee. Even if
you'd been up all night the night before, you'd find that you
would be walking on air. Gone would be your "tired feeling."
You'd get to that prospect if you had to crawl all the way
over to his office. You'd suddenly find that your will power —
your power to "get going" — had received a shot in the arm.
You'd be surprised at your own energy. Would you be afraid
or jittery? Would you be timid about approaching the prospect? Why be afraid when the outcome is certain?

Broaden Your "Look"

Well, no one is going to tell you that. But I can tell you something just as good: Your ultimate success is guaranteed if you will but *believe it* and get out there and make those calls. The same law will insure it that insures the big insurance companies and makes them the most stable, secure, "sure things" in the investment world — the law of averages.

I can tell you that your success is certain and guaranteed, just out there waiting for you, if you will broaden your "look" when you think of success. But if you would have this assurance, you must take your "look" off the individual trees and look at the woods. If you will picture in your mind's eye one aggregate "prospect" consisting of 100 individuals, then I can tell you in all good conscience: "This prospect is out there waiting to give you his business. He is all ready to to be signed up. You cannot fail to sell him, and there is absolutely nothing to be afraid of."

Broaden your look. Whenever you are tempted to fear the prospect, think of the "big prospect" consisting of 100 or more individuals. We *know* what this prospect will do. We *know* he will give you sufficient business to make you successful. There is no guesswork about him at all. His actions and behavior are the most predictable things in the world. It is because insurance companies can predict his actions right down to the fourth decimal point that insurance companies are "sure things."

POINTS TO REMEMBER

1. The next time you become jittery because selling is such a risky game, consider this: The risk that an insurance company takes on one individual policyholder is the most unpredictable thing in the world. What could be more risky than trying to guess when one certain individual is going to have an accident or become sick, or how long he is going to live? Yet, the insurance business itself is the most stable in the country, the safest investment anyone can make—the nearest thing to a "sure thing" in the way of guaranteed returns to investors. The risk an insurance company takes on one individual policyholder is tremen-

dous, yet the risk involved in 100,000 policyholders is so predictable it can be figured to the fourth decimal point.

2. Whether or not you will sell any single prospect is unpredictable. But do as the insurance companies do: "spread the risk" by seeing lots of prospects. Make enough calls, see enough prospects, and a number of sales are certain.

3. Adopt the attitude that "I've got nothing to lose" before making a call, instead of telling yourself, "Everything depends on this." Everything does not depend on *this*. You can strike out occasionally and still hit more home runs than anyone else in the league. Say to yourself, "If I don't call on this prospect, the sale is lost anyway. If I call on him and flop, I won't be any worse than I am now, so I've got nothing to lose."

15

HOW TO TURN TOUGH
CUSTOMERS INTO FRIENDS

YOU CAN'T JUDGE AN ACTIVE OR PASSIVE PER
sonality by the amount of noise a man makes or the amoun*
of dust he kicks up.

Not long ago I had a heart-to-heart talk with a young salesman who felt that he was not doing as well as he should.
When I pointed out that his life showed a pattern of passive-
ness, he denied it with a passion:

"If there is one thing that I am not, it is passive," he said.
"That has always been my big trouble. I'm not passive enough.
I don't take nothing from nobody. I've lost two good jobs
because of this, and I lose a good many sales today, just because if the prospect rubs me the wrong way or tries to lord
it over me, I blow my top."

"Did you plan to lose those two jobs?" I asked him. "Did
you *want* to lose your job?"

"No," he said, "of course not."

"And is it your own wish — is it a part of your plan and
goal — to lose sales by losing your temper? Is this what you
yourself actually want?"

"No," he said, "that certainly is not my idea of what I
want."

"Then you are allowing other people to dictate your course," I pointed out, "and you are passively following it. Your own goals, wants, and wishes are at the mercy of anyone who can make you lose your temper."

Two months later, I met this same salesman again and he said, "Dr. Brooks, that little talk we had together did me more good than anything that ever happened to me. I haven't lost my temper once since then; and on several occasions when a prospect has started out in a belligerent mood, I have kept my own goal in mind and gone on to sell him and leave him in a good humor."

This young man became more active, and, as he did so, he became less critical and argumentative. The greatest satisfaction that comes in life comes from overcoming one's problems — shaping one's environment, rather than allowing the environment to shape you. Passives do not know this satisfaction, because they will not act.

The passive's basic frustration and dissatisfaction comes from this chronic failure to *act*. They won't admit this, however, and pin their dissatisfaction on something outside themselves. They find fault with others. They like to prove others "wrong." Have you ever noticed that the man who is most critical of government is likely to be the man who doesn't even vote? The man who is most critical of the church is either a non-member or a passive member.

What Do You Want?

It is well sometimes to ask yourself the question, "What am I actually trying to do when I'm out here selling?"

If you want to fight—join the Marines.

If you want to argue—become a lawyer.

If you want to talk politics—run for office.

If you want to convince everyone how much smarter you are than he is; if your desire is to put everyone in his place—then you'd better find a wife who can support you and give up all work and enjoy your hobby.

But if your desire is to sell, and get orders, then don't get sidetracked. Don't fight the customer!

Unless you are selling campaign buttons, it is not necessary to qualify a prospect on politics before selling him. Unless you are selling books on theology, it is not necessary to qualify a prospect on religion in order to sell him. Steer clear of controversial subjects that may lead to arguments.

Three Rules for Cooling off Angry Prospects

It is inexcusable for any salesman to ever *start* an argument. However, I know from experience that sometimes a salesman finds a prospect already "mad." A previous unpleasant experience with another salesman; dissatisfaction experienced with your product in the past; any number of things may have a prospect "conditioned" like a live fuse, ready to blow up the minute you announce you are a salesman. Over the years, I worked out three simple rules for dealing with this type of prospect.

1. Let the Prospect Blow off Steam

When there is too much steam on a boiler, there is but one thing to do: Let the steam off. When the safety valve begins to let it off, do nothing to interfere. If you try to shut off the escaping steam, you'll only risk a big explosion by blowing up the entire boiler. The chances are that something has been "building up" inside the angry prospect for weeks — perhaps for years. He hasn't had an outlet for it until you come along. Unwittingly, you have temporarily increased the pressure and caused the safety plug to blow out. But if you are patient and wait for the steam to blow itself out, it will eventually do so.

You then have the prospect at a psychological disadvantage. For if you do nothing to interfere once his steam starts escaping, it will *all* come out. He will be left without *any emotional power* whatsoever. He will have spent himself. His resistance to your ideas will be at an abnormally low ebb. He will be like a boxer who, in a wild flurry, literally "punches himself out" and becomes so arm-weary from throwing punches that he is then all but helpless before his opponent.

2. Agree with Him

Opposition builds up emotional power. Agreement disarms

it. Try sitting calmly and nodding your head in agreement with the angry prospect, and notice how it seems to take away his power. It is best, especially in the early part of the interview, not to interrupt the prospect, but you can nod your head silently in agreement.

When he pauses for breath, you may say something like this: "Yes, I can certainly see that it would *seem* that way to you . . ." or, "Under the circumstances, I can certainly understand why you feel that way. . . ." Later, when the prospect has spent himself and it is time for you to start talking, you can still agree: "You are right — however, you overlooked one thing . . .," or, "I agree with you in every particular except this one."

Agreement helps to get you on the prospect's side. It is difficult to keep thinking of a person as an "enemy" who keeps agreeing with everything you say.

Another thing that helps the prospect to think of you as a friend instead of an enemy is to get him to do you some small favor. We tend to feel the way we act, just as we act in accordance to our feelings. Get the prospect to acting like a friend, and it will help him feel friendly. "Can I have a drink of water?" "May I sit down?" — anything, as long as it makes him act as a friend would act.

Leonard Fields, our Knoxville Branch Manager of Union Bankers Insurance Company told me not long ago how he had called on a prospect through error. Someone had sent the "lead" in as a joke. When Fields went out, he found he was calling on a wealthy retired railroad man, who lived in a fine house. When Leonard was about ten feet from the door, the prospect suddenly opened the door and said, "If you are an insurance salesman, stop right there — that's as far as any insurance man ever gets."

"Mr. *X*," said Leonard, "May I sit down here on your front steps and remove a stone from my shoe?" He said he didn't mind, and Leonard slowly removed his shoe. "As I did so," he says, "I commented that he must spend a lot of money to keep his grounds so beautiful. He took great pride in doing his own work around the house and informed me of the fact in no uncertain terms. I began to ask about different shrubs and flowers — and he seemed to forget who I was. Finally, after some time, I told him he was obviously a successful businessman and I would like to explain a very good investment to him.

"He said, 'Well, I like you; if you want to waste more of your time, go ahead.' One hour later, I left with a large application."

3. A Soft Answer Turns Wrath to Your Own Advantage

There is an old proverb among certain savage tribes that when you hurl your spear at an enemy and fail to hit him, it returns to strike your own breast. It is a psychological fact that, when wrath or hatred fails to find a responsive target, it becomes impotent. To find a satisfactory outlet, rage and all other emotions must find a *responsive* target. In other words, rage must encounter resistance and opposition, in order to score a "hit." It cannot touch you if you yourself remain unresponsive.

Perhaps this is what wise old King Solomon had in mind when he said that "A soft answer *turns away* wrath." It turns the arrows in their flight. Somehow the person who is raging knows this, and his failure to hit the target leaves him feeling helpless. His initial feeling of rage is likely to be replaced by a feeling of apology. He somehow feels psychologically *obligated* to the other person.

The purpose of emotion, said Prescott Lecky and other psychologists, is to furnish extra power to combat and overcome difficulties and obstacles. But when it meets with no difficulty — no opposition — no obstacle, it tends to evaporate.

I have seen this happen time and time again. Not long ago I was in an office where a sales manager called in a salesman to "chew him out." The salesman had blundered.

"What in the hell were you thinking of?" began the sales manager. "Don't you ever use your head? That was the dumbest thing I have ever seen."

The salesman stood quietly and said nothing. His face never

changed expression. "Well, don't just stand there — what *is* your explanation?" said his boss.

"I have no explanation," said the salesman, "except just what you said. It was just a dumb blunder."

Well, it was the sales manager now who was confused and ill at ease. He began to shuffle papers on his desk self-consciously. "I'm sorry," said the salesman, "I should have known better."

"Well, I don't know," said the boss. "We all make mistakes. Don't worry about it. Go on out and do the best you can."

The Three Rules in Action

W. C. Eason, one of our District Managers, tells me that his most interesting sales experiences have been these "hot-in-the-collar" type prospects that most salesmen dread.

Selling the tough ones is more fun. This is not surprising, for it is always the fish that puts up some fight, the golf course that offers some difficulties, that give us the biggest "kick." Mr. Eason says that his most interesting sales experience came several years ago when he was working for another insurance company. The following is the story in his own words:

"I had a lead card on an elderly lady a few miles east of San Angelo, Texas. Going out to her ranch, I came to a mail box that had the same name on it as the lead card, and I turned in the driveway. When I rang the bell, a young lady in her late twenties came to the door. I introduced myself and the company as usual and, after exchanging a few words, soon found out I was at the wrong house. Not passing up any bets, I asked if she and her husband had hospitalization insurance. She said 'no.'

"By this time, her husband had walked to the door, and he asked what company I represented. When I told him, it was just as if I had pulled a trigger. To say his language was abusive is an understatement. He cursed, snorted, ranted, and raved. *I let him blow off steam for a full 20 minutes, during which time I did not say a word.* He and his wife had had a policy two years previously and had lost it while doing some remodeling work on their house. He had written to the home office, asking them to send a new policy by return mail. The duplicate policy did not come by return mail, but by coincidence, a premium notice did. He thought he had been mistreated and did not renew his policy.

"After 20 minutes be began to slow down, and *I told him that I was sorry* that he had this unpleasant experience. I sympathized with him and told him I could understand how he felt the way he did — however, I *explained* to him that an insurance policy was a legal document, and that for his own protection, a certain legal process had to be gone through with in order to issue a new policy. I explained to him that the policy could not have been returned to him by return air mail.

"All this time we had been standing at his door. *I asked if I might come in and sit down.* He asked me to come in, but warned me that he would buy under no condition.

"However, *he apparently felt obligated to listen,* and he was one of the most attentive prospects I have ever talked with. He seemed to have spent all his resistance on the front steps. After about an hour, he was agreeing with me that my hospitalization plan was as good as, if not a little better than, any plan he had seen. I had sold him on the plan.

"The next step was to show him his need for hospitalization. I was also successful in arousing a desire on his part to want the plan. The one thing standing in the way of a sale was the prospect's previous commitment that he was *not* going to buy. He needed to save face. However, *I* had not mentioned this during the entire interview, and he had not mentioned it again. I had not argued against his flat-footed stand "not to buy," but had ignored it and concentrated on putting my ideas across.

"I decided that the best course to follow was just to not bring up the subject again — to pretend that it had never happened. I took my pen from my pocket, and asked him if he wanted full coverage on both of them. He wanted to know how much it would cost them annually and I told him the amount of annual premium. He told me to write out the applications."

Yes—But

You can avoid many arguments if you will employ the "yes-but" technique. Notice how Eason agreed with the prospect — *but* explained to him why the policy could not have been issued immediately by return mail.

I remember one instance where I called upon a young fellow about twenty-five years of age and attempted to interest him in a $5,000 life-insurance policy. He owned a small grocery store in the city of Lufkin, Texas. He had a great respect for his father. Several times he mentioned that his father had made a success of this business, and I sensed his admiration. He asked me to come back the next day. When I did, he stated that he wouldn't be interested in the policy because he had "talked it over with father" the night before. His father had suggested that the best thing for him to do was to put this money into the grocery store and let the insurance go at this time.

It would have been easy to have argued with him. It would have been easy to have said, "Can't you think for yourself? Do you still have to get permission from your father before you can do anything?" But this would not have gotten the order.

"I am sure your father is sincere, and that he is advising you for the best," I said. "He feels you can make more with the money if you put it into the business here. Your father has made a big success in the grocery business in the past. He is ready and willing to take care of your business, run the store again, and take care of your widow, should anything happen to you. I am sure he could do it, and would be perfectly willing to do it. . . .

"*But* a thought that occurred to me is this: Your father is almost seventy years of age, and if anything should happen to *him* — who would then take care of the store?" The young man gave this some thought, and agreed that his father had probably not thought about "this important part of the problem." I ended up writing him the policy.

Often, you will find that the *very thing* that seems to stand in the way of a sale can be used to make the sale; the thing that seems to bar the sale can be used as a lever to move the prospect. The door that seems to shut in your face can be made to "swing" the sale, but never if you try to batter it down by force of argument.

Judge, Jury, and Defendant Rolled into One

Never put yourself in direct opposition to the prospect. Never argue with the prospect. Lawyers win cases by argument — salesman, never.

The reason is simple. The lawyer often makes a fool out of the defendant, by sharp wit. *But the defendant doesn't decide the case.*

The lawyer "argues with" the opposing lawyer until he is blue in the face. He shouts. He stamps his feet and waves his arms. *But the opposing lawyer is not the man who will pass sentence in the case.*

The lawyer argues his case *before* a jury — but have you ever heard a lawyer argue *with* a jury?

The lawyer pleads with the judge — and tells him how wrong the opposing lawyer is — but have you ever heard a lawyer tell a judge how wrong the judge is?

It is well to remember that, in selling, the prospect is defendant, judge, opposing counsel, and jury all rolled into one. You can't "whup" him — and, as General Nathan Bedford Forrest once expressed it, the only sensible thing to do is "join him."

POINTS TO REMEMBER

1. Keep in mind what you really want. Is it to win a fight, to win a debate, or to show off your own importance? Or is it *to make a sale?* If your purpose is to make a sale, avoid these other things that would interfere.

2. Cool down angry prospects by letting them blow off steam, by agreeing with them, and by giving only "soft" answers.

3. Get the hostile prospect to act like a friend, and soon he will feel friendly. Ask some small favor. "May I sit down"? "Could I have a drink of water?"

4. When you must finally disagree with the prospect, use the "Yes, but —" technique. "Yes, you are right about that Mr. Jones, but—." "Yes, I can see your point, but have you considered this—?"

5. Lawyers can win cases by argument—salesmen can't. The lawyer argues *before* a jury, but never *with* a jury. He tries to make a fool of the opposing counsel and show the defendant up, but he never tries to make a fool of the judge. No lawyer could win a case by argument if judge, jury, opposing counsel, and defendant were all the same person. This is exactly why the salesman can't win with argument. In selling, the prospect *is* judge, jury, defendant, and opposing counsel— all rolled into one.

16

WHY
"SIMPLE SIMON SALESMEN"
NEVER GET A STRIKE

THE FIRST THING A GOOD FISHERMAN WANTS to know is what kind of waters he is fishing in. What sort of fish are there below the surface? Which are biting best now? What bait is most successful?

He knows that it does no good to fish for trout if there are only catfish in the waters. He knows that just because there is water this does not mean that there are "prospects" for successful fishing. He also knows that just because there are "fish" there does not mean that any kind of bait will catch them.

Simple Simon went fishing in a pail of water, it is true; but then, he was Simple Simon.

Simple Simon's fault wasn't that he did not fish hard enough, or did not use good bait or fine tackle. His one mistake was that he did not take the trouble to "qualify" the waters he was fishing in. Simple Simon was a passive.

To a passive it is too much trouble — to much effort — to do a little planning, a little exploring. It is simpler just to drop in your hook and hope a big fish will come along and hang himself on it. Like other passives, Simple Simon probably said to himself, "The fish probably aren't biting today anyway, and after all, what can I *do* — I can't *make* them bite."

Simple Simon Salesmen

Unfortunately, many salesmen are like Simple Simon. They do not take the trouble of finding out what ideas, wants, desires, hungers, dreams are swimming around unseen in the prospect's mind. Their salesmanship may be flawless, but they catch no fish. They bait their hooks for bass, when the only fish in the waters are tuna. I have found that good fishermen usually make good salesmen. Perhaps it is no coincidence that Jesus selected fishermen as the men to spread His message and convince others of His truths. There is a lot in common between fishing and selling.

What Are Prospects?

W. B. Stadler, our District Manager in Roanoke, Virginia, has a saying, "The Suspect becomes a Prospect only when you learn something about what lies beneath the surface of his personality."

Remember my experience, related in Chapter 9, where the prospect wasn't interested in my appeals to his devotion to his wife, or any of the other ordinary appeals, and how, at long last, I found out that the man was then contemplating a divorce and wanted to make sure that his wife did *not* get any benefits?

That experience has been worth a lot to me. I almost lost an easy sale by being a Simple Simon. I was using the customary "bait" and not getting any nibbles. The fish I was fishing for just weren't there.

But when I found that this man *was* interested in providing for his children, it was an easy sale. Looking back on this experience, I could see that there were many signs, and plenty of clues, that should have alerted me to the true state of affairs between the man and his wife. The way he frowned slightly and looked uncomfortable when I complimented him on his devotion to his wife; the coldness between them, and a dozen other signals that I missed, simply because I had a preconceived idea of the kind of fish that were supposed to be there and was blind to everything else.

Watch for the Bounce

Another sign that should have alerted me was the fact that there was absolutely no response to my sales talk. Any time your "pitch" is hitting home, you will get a bounce-back. Sometimes the prospect agrees. Sometimes he disagrees — or appears to, in order to encourage you to convince him of his own doubts.

Francis Ewton, Florida State Manager of Nablico, says, "As long as the prospect keeps coming up with objections, then we don't have too much to worry about; but, brother, when he clams up and won't say anything, we're in trouble."

Many of our development managers as well as persons in the real estate and banking interests with whom I am associated, find that a direct question can be used in obtaining a definite "sounding" of the prospect.

Joe F. Luker, one of our regional directors, says that when he is in the process of a sale and he cannot obtain any definite response as to which type of hospitalization the prospect likes best, he simply lays out before his prospects the several different sales sheets explaining the several types of hospital protection and says, "Which of these plans do you think would fit into your budget best?" He employs the strategy of the fisherman who finds himself in strange waters and throws out a half dozen different types of bait to see what kind of fish are beneath the surface.

The Secret of the Successful Recruiter

Tom High, Agency Director of Union Bankers Insurance Company, is one of our most successful men when it comes to recruiting new salesmen and managers, an important phase of work for any sales director. Not long ago he told me how he finally "landed" an outstanding young man he had had his eye on for many months.

"Dr. Brooks," he said, "I tried three times to sell this young man on coming with our firm. Since all the polls show that young men are "security-conscious" today, I tried to touch his hunger for security. I pointed out to him the *stability* of our company. I showed him facts and figures to support my pitch. I showed him articles in trade papers predicting that our company was destined to become one of the leaders in the entire nation. I also concentrated on the steady income he could count on. Another "pitch" I used was "easy work." I pointed out our program for the home office helping the salesman and working with him — furnishing him with leads; how our claims department processed claims and paid them in an average of 24 hours, thus creating good will among our clients and creating new business; how our policies were simply worded, easily understood by the prospect, with no double-talk in fine print to embarrass a salesman. I told him how he could actually share in the profits of the company through our profit-sharing stock-ownership plan. And I got absolutely nowhere. There was simply no power in my pitch — and I knew that something was wrong.

"The next time I met this young man, I did less talking and more listening. I asked leading questions. Gradually, I began to see what I thought the trouble was. This young man was not interested in *security* — he was interested in *opportunity*.

"I changed my pitch entirely. I pointed out to him how one salesman had started with our company only two years ago and was now state director. I named the names of a dozen men who had started with us at the bottom and had risen through the ranks to top executive positions. I pointed out that this was an important part of our company policy. The result was that this young man came with our organization, is making twice as much money as he was before, and gives every promise that he is on the way to the top."

Give Them What They Want

I know an old fisherman down in Galveston who insists on using cornbread and bacon grease for bait. It is his "favorite" bait. He used it with success when he was a boy, fishing in the creek behind his house. He catches no fish today, but he still insists on using the same "favorite" bait. The fish "ought" to bite it, and he cannot understand why they do not.

Many insurance salesmen have "favorite" policies, just as the old fisherman has his favorite bait. With one it may be ordinary life; with another, mortgage insurance; with another, retirement income. The result is that, when such a salesman meets a prospect who is already 90 per cent sold on a different type policy, he must do a 190 per cent selling job if he gets the order. He must first *unsell* the prospect on the policy he wants, then *sell* him a different one. Sometimes he unsells him on insurance altogether.

It is good for the salesman to advise, educate, and counsel — *when the prospect asks for advice.* But only a Simple Simon says, "Oh, my goodness you don't want that — I've got something much better than that," when a prospect leads off with, "For a long time I've been planning on buying an endowment policy."

Simple Simons aren't limited to the insurance field. Not long ago I overheard a conversation between a prospect and a real estate salesman:

Prospect: "My wife and I have been planning and saving for years. We have our home all planned. We want a stone house. . ."

Salesman: "Never buy a stone house. They are hard to heat and will sweat in hot weather."

Prospect: "We've got our heart set on that new type panel heating. . ."

Salesman: "Personally, I do not believe you can beat steam heat. A lot of this newfangled stuff isn't satisfactory."

The conversation went on in that vein for ten minutes, until the prospect excused himself. I often wondered whether he ever built *any* type of house.

In contrast to the Simple-Simon selling technique cited above, I happened to be visiting one of our sub-division companies, the Western United Realty Company in Houston not long ago. A prospect came in and approached Mr. D. A. Terry, president of the firm.

Mr. Terry began telling about a new subdivision and the

beautiful lots where the prospect and his wife would have the "joy of seeing your dreams take shape as you build your own home just as you want it."

"I'm not interested in purchasing a vacant lot and later having to build my home on this property. What I'm interested in is a completed, new home, which will eliminate the necessity of building and going through this detail."

With this much of a clue, Mr. Terry began to sound him out still further by asking questions which would bring out *exactly* what the prospect wanted. How many were in his family? Did he want a two-story or one-story house? What type architecture did he prefer? Did he like ranch types? Mr. Terry literally played a game of "Twenty Questions" with this prospect until he guessed his "secret." The sale was consummated that same afternoon. It was always "what do *you* want?" — never "this is what I'd like to sell you."

Timing Is Important

Timing is important. The power salesman must know when to "sell hard" and when to "sell easy." Like an expert fisherman, he knows when he must allow the fish to "run" with the line, and when to start reeling in. If he reels in too fast, or too suddenly, the fish may break the line and get away. If he never reels in at all, he never lands the fish. There is but one way the fisherman can tell when to do what — he must "qualify" his fish.

Don't Disqualify the Prospect

A prospect walks into an automobile agency that sells a $3,500 automobile and a $2,000 automobile. It so happens this prospect can barely buy the $2,000 car. It is impossible for him even to make the down payment on the $3,500 car. But a Simple Simon salesman doesn't bother to find this out. He is anxious to make a "big sale." He takes the prospect for a ride in the $3,500 car. Finally, the prospect admits apologetically that he *cannot* buy the more expensive car and that he wants to take a look at the cheaper one. He looks at it. But now it doesn't look like much. He is comparing it with the car he can't buy — and he doesn't like it. Had he seen it first, it would have looked good. Now he sees only all the things it doesn't have. He leaves without buying any kind of car.

Many real estate sales are lost the same way. A couple have decided to buy a new home. They *can* buy a $15,000 house, but the salesman doesn't qualify them as to price and makes the mistake of showing them his newest $40,000 dream home, which "has everything." Finally the salesman discovers his error and shows them his latest $15,000 "budget home." But in their mind's eye they are still looking at the dream house. And the budget home, in comparison, is disappointing. Either they do not buy at all, or else they buy the budget house and become dissatisfied customers.

My son, R. P. Brooks, who is vice-president of Nablico, read over the first draft of this chapter and said, "It is certainly true that many sales are lost because we have failed to make a price qualification during the early part of the interview. If I feel that possibly the customer may not be in a position financially to meet and pay for the program I have in mind, I ask, 'Could you invest $15 per month or $45 quarterly in a gold mine or an oil well?' If he says 'yes,' at least I know that he *can* pay that much if I can convince him that insurance is a good investment. If he says 'no,' I know that I am overshooting the mark on price."

Appearances Are Deceiving

G. M. Whitten, State Manager of Nablico in Arkansas, was out working with a new salesman. Whitten, wise in the ways of sales managers, knew that one graphic experience would teach more than months of lectures. Whitten drove out into a rural section and pulled up in front of a dilapidated farm house, with "cracks so big in the walls you could throw your shoes through them."

"What are we stopping here for?" asked the new salesman.

Whitten ignored the question and they went to the front door. They were met by a barefoot farmer with a big cud of tobacco in his jaw. Whitten went inside and began his pitch. The only other sound was the "ping" as the farmer hit a tin can in the corner at regular intervals with tobacco juice.

The new salesman became embarrassed. "For pete's sake," he said to Whitten, "let's give the fellow a policy and go home."

Whitten continued his pitch. What the new salesman didn't know was that Whitten had previously "qualified" this prospect. He had learned through others in the community that the old farmer "had the first dollar he ever earned" and that he prided himself on "paying cash on the barrelhead." His close was geared to this advance qualifying. When the farmer asked, "Feller, how much does that thing cost?" Whitten quoted him the *monthly* price, and explained he could buy it *on time*.

"Shucks," said the farmer, "I won't fool with that damn stuff every month, how much is it by the year?"

Whitten told him, and the farmer said, "Mama, get this fellow some money."

His wife came in with a large old-fashioned purse and counted out $103.50 from a roll that showed "plenty more where that came from."

W. E. Goare, one of our managers, tells of a similar experience. He passed a home in a rural section that hardly appeared lived-in. Weeds were growing all over the yard, and the house was dilapidated. With some misgivings, he knocked on the door and found a bachelor who was not interested in housekeeping or pretty yards, but was very much concerned with his security.

"Without too much trouble I sold him a hospital contract and a life contract and netted myself $50 commission. The sale itself was not large, but it has been worth a lot to me for it taught me not to pass up any bets merely on surface appearances."

Never disqualify a prospect on appearances. Appearances are only the surface of the water. The fish are always down underneath—and sometimes the biggest fish are found in the most unlikely looking waters. It's what's beneath the surface that counts—and that's what you must somehow find out about, if you are going to be a power salesman.

You Can Sell Ice Boxes to Eskimos!

Despite the old saying "You can't sell ice boxes to Eskimos," Jim Moran, the promotion expert, did it on a dare. Moran, who attained world-wide fame (and fortune) by always doing the *spectacular*—such as looking for a needle in a haystack in a large city—announced several years ago he was on his way to Alaska to sell ice boxes to Eskimos.

Moran was successful because of a shrewd piece of "qualifying." He didn't try to sell the ice boxes on the basis of how they would keep food cold, preserve food, or any of the usual sales points. He knew this bait would not work. It touched no need of the Eskimos. Moran asked himself what *did* Eskimos need, and how could his product possibly be tied in to that need. The following is the sentence he used:

"These boxes are insulated, and will keep your food from freezing hard."

Why Women Wouldn't Buy Shirts

Elmer Wheeler, the "sizzle salesman," got his start as a sales counselor many years ago when he was a space salesman for a Baltimore newspaper.

May's Department Store had given him an ad for men's shirts. Elmer came around the next day, and Mr. May told him, "Your ad is no good—the shirts aren't selling."

"Looks like there are plenty of women around the shirt counter," said Elmer.

"Yes, but they are just lookers; none of them is buying."

Elmer went over and listened in on the sales pitch the clerks were making to the women lookers. They were telling how these shirts were form-fitting, how they were tailored better, how the collars wouldn't choke and the tails wouldn't come out. This was all bait that would appeal to *men*. The shoppers were *women*.

Elmer picked up a shirt, examined it closely and noticed

that these shirts had the buttons sewed on with triple-strength thread. Holding up a shirt, he said, "Ladies, these buttons are anchored on, and will not come off in the wringer!" As he said this he dramatically held up a shirt and gave a big yank on a button, to show how well it was anchored on.

This appeal started a stampede to the shirt counter that did not end until every last single shirt was sold out—the first time such a thing had happened in the store's history!

Elmer told me one day,—"Pierce, whether you're selling insurance or can-openers, automobiles or men's shirts—there is power in qualifying the prospect."

A Sales Secret That's Been Tested for Thousands of Years

The Sales Secret in this chapter has been used by power salesmen for thousands of years. St. Paul, that power salesman for Christianity, said that he offered milk for babes and meat for adults. And if archeologists ever dig up an old sales manual in an Egyptian tomb, they will doubtless find that men who used POWER SELLING in ancient Egypt recommended baiting your hook with the bait appropriate to the fish you were trying to catch.

Remember that Simple Simon's one big fault was not that he did not have good bait, not that he did not have expensive fishing equipment, not that he lacked skill in "landing" fish.

His one big fault was that he just failed to take the trouble to find out what kind of fish, if any, were down there beneath the surface.

POINTS TO REMEMBER

1. Salesmanship is similar to fishing. If you would be successful, your bait must be selected according to what sort of fish are there. Surface appearances are not important. The fish, the ideas that are underneath the surface, are what count.

2. Find out the real ideas, wants, hungers, dreams, that are underneath the surface. Then use bait that will feed *them*.

3. When you get some kind of response, you know you are on the right

track. When you get a "bounce back," you know your pitch is hitting home.

4. When you get no nibbles at all, when the prospect doesn't even make a half way strike occasionally—change your bait.

5. You must give them what *they* want, not what you would like them to have.

17

PUTTING "GUTS" IN YOUR SELLING

Pressure selling is a subject that is not often written about. Back around the turn of the century, books on "How to Have a Dominant Personality," "How to Force People to Do What You Want," and so forth, became a fad. These books, which had as their dominant theme how to be superior to others and force other people to do things by will power, had a distinct influence on salesmanship. In many quarters, salesmanship came to be regarded as a *contest*, in which the "stronger personality" won. Getting the order was equivalent to defeating the prospect. Techniques were devised to force prospects into buying, without any regard for arousing a desire within the prospect.

These methods came to be known generally as *high-pressure selling*. They came into disfavor for two reasons: (1) they did not work, and (2) prospects resented them. An inevitable reaction set in, and all types of pressure selling became taboo. Salesmen were taught never to use harsh words, never to make the prospect uncomfortable, never to "back the hearse up to the door."

Outside and Inside Pressure

Good salesmen of all times, however, without regard for fads, have always used *inside pressure* and have avoided *outside pressure*. Outside pressure is an attempt to *make* people do things. Inside pressure makes people *want* to do things.

Jesus was the best salesman, if I may use this term, of all times. He never forced anyone to listen to him. He never tried to convince anyone by force or threats. He always attempted to arouse a desire within his listeners for a better life. To the simple folk, who realized their need for a better life, his words were gentle. But to the Pharisees, who were perfectly satisfied with their righteousness, he used words more harsh than any salesman would use today, in order to shock them into a realization of the predicament they were in. To those who were convinced of their goodness and saw no need to change, he announced that harlots would go into the Kingdom of Heaven before them!

Why we do what we do. Many psychologists assert that the only reason we do anything at all is to escape pressure and tension. For example, hunger creates tension and pressure. You seek food as a means of relieving the tension. You eat a big meal—and relax. Anytime you desire anything, your very desire creates certain inner tension or pressure. This inner tension or pressure causes you to act. Without some pressure from the inside, you feel no need to act. You are satisfied and content with things as they are.

All real salesmen are "dissatisfiers." Unless you can make the prospect feel dissatisfied with what he's got, he is not going to act to sign on the dotted line. If you are going to arouse a desire in a prospect, you are going to use pressure, for you cannot have desire without pressure. Many times, you will find the prospect asleep to his real needs, and it becomes necessary to wake him up before a desire can be created. You are sometimes going to have to use plain words that tell the unvarnished truth.

One way that human beings have of remaining satisfied is to avoid the truth of the predicament they are in. They ra-

tionalize, which is simply telling oneself "rational lies." There
is the drunkard, for example, who tells himself, "I can quit
anytime I want to." There is the failure, who tells himself,
"I am not interested in anything as materialistic as money."

All of us tend to gloss over unpleasant or painful things in
life, by using pretty, "sugar-coated" words to describe them.
The only trouble with sugar-coated words is that they keep
us from seeing the crisis situation we are in, and we feel no
inward pressure to change things. "Death" is not a pretty
word. Few of us like to use it or even think about it. We
had much rather refer to it as "passing on" or "if anything
should happen to me." Leaving one's wife and children penni-
less is not a pretty picture. It is unpleasant—but it is a reality.
Many prospects manage to feel perfectly satisfied in this regard, simply because they will not think about it at all. And
it is sometimes necessary literally to "back the hearse up to
the door" in order to make the crisis real to them.

Pointing out inconsistencies. The late Dr. Prescott Lecky
said that you do not need to worry about *making* people act
on a certain idea if you can simply demonstrate to them that
the idea is *inconsistent* with other ideas or standards they hold.
Once you demonstrate that a certain idea is inconsistent, the
person literally *must* reject it and act in accordance with that
rejection. The strongest force in human personality, he said,
was the urge to preserve the "integrity of the organization" to
keep all our ideas consistent with each other. The reason so
many of us are able to harbor ideas that are inconsistent with
each other is that we never see them bare-faced and recognize
them for what they are. Instead we rationalize them—we
sugar-coat them, and try to distort them to make them com-
patible.

Once you unmask one of these inconsistencies, however, and
show it up in its true colors, you do not need to worry about
applying pressure on the subject from the outside. You do
not need to exhort or preach or scold. You will have created
a pressure inside the person that is much more effective than
any external pressure could ever be.

Lecky gained wide attention by "curing" stutterers, nail

biters, and poor spellers among students. He did this by literally "selling" the student. He pointed out that the standard responsible for the social defect was *inconsistent* with other strong standards held by the student. Once the student himself saw this and accepted it, he was literally forced to change himself.

For example, Lecky "cured" poor spellers by showing them that the "standard" responsible for their poor spelling was inconsistent with another "standard." "You have accepted yourself as a poor speller—and that has become your standard. But you expect to get by in spite of your poor spelling. You expect other people to excuse you. You are like a beggar going around with his hand out—begging for indulgence."

Use Standards to Create Inner Pressure in Your Prospects

Most married men maintain the standard "I love my wife and family," and secure ego satisfaction from the standard, "I am able to provide for my family and protect them." If you can show that these standards are in conflict with the idea that "I don't believe in insurance" or "I don't need insurance," the prospect will almost sell himself.

Sales sentences that create inner pressure. Here are sentences that point out this conflict and build an inner pressure:

Prospect: I may pay for this A. & H. policy for 15 years and never have an accident.

Salesman: True, and I hope you never need it. You are right in saying that it is a gamble. No one knows whether you will have an accident or become sick. But you are taking that gamble whether you buy this policy or not. If you don't have this policy you are taking still another risk: that your wife and children may not have money for food and clothes should your income be suddenly cut off. That is one gamble we do not need to take. It is a gamble no man has a right to take, because the stakes involved are too high: whether or not your children will go hungry or be denied the things they need."

Salesman: "What would happen to your family if your expenses increased $200 per month for the next six months?"

Salesman: "If you had to miss 25 or 50 paydays, would it make any difference to your wife and family?"

Salesman: "I can tell you how much this policy will cost you—but no one on earth can tell you how much it will cost your family if you don't have it."

Salesman: "It's your job to provide a living for your wife and family—but your are not fully providing for them, unless you are prepared to provide for them at all times."

Salesman: "When your wife married you, she agreed to stick with you 'in sickness and in health.' It is only fair that you live up to your part of the bargain and be prepared to provide for her 'in sickness' as well as when you are in health."

These same standards can be used to sell any number of other products.

"Mr. Jones, every girl dreams of growing up, getting married to a man who can take care of her, and becoming a 'homemaker.' But she cannot become a homemaker if she doesn't have a home. Every woman dreams of having a home of her own."

I know a cookware salesman who frequently has no trouble selling the lady of the house on his products, for she realizes the need of them. The big bottleneck is the husband, who protests that "it costs too much." He uses this technique:

Salesman: "Mr. Jones, when you eat out, you probably tip the waitress at least ten cents. Is that correct?"

Mr. Jones: "Yes."

Salesman: "Well, if you would just leave a dime by your plate for your wife in the morning and again in the evening—that 20 cents a day would buy this cookware that she needs and wants."

To say "no," the husband has to literally admit in front of his wife that he thinks more of the waitress than he does of her.

Another standard that most of us have is the standard that we are thrifty; that we do not wilfully destroy things. Salesmen who sell equipment that produces more efficiency and saves the prospect money can point up the inconsistency of *not* having their product in a spectacular fashion, by saying, "Mr. Brown, every month that you keep this old, outmoded machine you might as well take ten ten-dollar bills and light your cigars with them."

How to Use Shock Treatments on Your Prospects

Shock treatments are widely used today in psychiatry. No adequate theory has ever explained just why they work. But a doctor friend of mine tells me that he believes these shock treatments work for the same reason that the frog will suddenly jump out of the pan if boiling water is added.

"Many mental patients," he says, "have let their constructive, life-giving instincts become gradually strangled by the destructive or death-wish tendencies. They have gradually given up the struggle and the 'will to live.' They embrace self-destruction and death a little at a time. But when an electric shock treatment is given, they experience in reality what amounts to a short coma very similar to real death. When they are thus brought face to face with real death, their own constructive and life-giving impulses spring into action and cure them."

Salesmen, too, can use "shock treatments," sometimes with good results. Sometimes in addressing a sales meeting, I take a thousand-dollar bill from my pocket and hold it up. "Some salesman in this room lost this thousand-dollar bill", I announce. All at once everyone in the room is all ears. "Yes," I say, "some salesman in this room lost this thousand-dollar bill last month—by not putting in eight productive hours of selling per day, by being too lazy to take the trouble to arouse desire, or by neglecting some other fundamental of salesmanship."

The effect is always much more impressive than if I merely say, "You fellows ought to get out and work a little harder— if you would, you'd make more money."

How motorists were sold on safety. When I first became president of the Texas Safety Council, I suggested that we use the "shock treatment" on motorists to sell them on driving more carefully. I recommended that our highway signs be changed as follows:

WAS	CHANGED TO
Drive Slowly	Speed Kills
Drive Carefully and Save a Life	Don't Kill—Drive Carefully
Sharp Curve—Drive Carefully	Death Lurks Around This Curve
Drive with Care, Children Playing	Don't MURDER Our Children.

Another suggestion I made was that we put up markers showing how many people had been killed on certain curves, and that wrecked cars be placed by the side of the road to warn the motorist that "This could happen to you!"

These signs made some people unhappy. But they did prove to be more effective than the old sugar-coated signs, and today the "harsh words" technique is used by safety councils throughout the country. And for the past several years, Dallas, Texas, has held the record as the Safest City in the United States.

Make It Hot for Your Prospect

Not long ago I was talking to Mr. Russ Rosson, Central Texas Regional Director for National Bankers Life Insurance Company. "Dr. Brooks," he said, "some time ago I heard you make a talk on having guts enough to bring up unpleasant subjects. At the time I was trying to sell a 53-year old man a life policy, and wasn't getting very far. After hearing your talk, I went back to my prospect and said, 'Mr. X, old age may seem to *some people* a long way off, and it probably is. But sometimes, when we begin to reach an evening time in life and it appears to be not very far away, then it is probably too late to take out the protection you need!'"

"That statement must have registered, because he began to wonder, I think, whether he would be insurable or whether it would be "too late' when he did decide to buy this protection for himself and family. I came away with a $10,000 sale that I would have lost had I not had guts enough to talk about a very unpleasant subject—old age."

Remember the frog in the story, who saw no need to jump

as long as the hot water was added to the pan gradually and always seemed merely warm? Luke-warm words have the same effect on prospects. They see no need to change, because they can always tolerate the luke-warm water the salesman adds to the pan. Sometimes the only way you can get a man to act or move is to "make it hot for him" where he is. Pussy-footing and sugar-coated words will not do this.

As long as he is telling the truth and believes in the worth of his product, it is no more "unethical" for a salesman to put a prospect in "hot water" than it is for an evangelist or a doctor—both of whom get people to act by painting to them a painful word picture of *what will happen if they don't.*

Personally, I believe in insurance. I believe that it is a matter of life-and-death importance. And because I do believe in it, I have no more scruples against telling the prospect the truth about what will happen to his family if he doesn't have adequate coverage than I would have about telling a friend what will happen to him if he doesn't come out of a burning house.

Many times I have had prospects tell me, "I cannot decide now" or "I am not ready to decide now."

"Mr. Jones," I say, "You cannot keep from making a decision. You are making a decision today, whether you want to or not. If you decide *not* to have this protection, you are deciding that you are going to leave the welfare of your wife and children to luck, chance, or charity."

I have never yet had a man to resent my telling him that. I can say it and get by with it because I believe it and I feel it.

A. E. Willson, Jr., district manager for Union Bankers Insurance Company, had a prospect who had "too many bills already" to add to them by taking out accident and health insurance. The prospect had a son who had a paper route. Willson said, "Mr. Prospect, with all these bills you have to pay, what would happen if someone came running in and told you that your son had been hit by a car and was being taken to the hospital? Suppose, in the excitement, someone bumps into this kerosene stove and upsets a boiling pot of coffee on one of your smaller children. What would you do? How would you pay your bills then? Perhaps I've exaggerated a little bit. These things may never happen, and I hope they don't— but if and when an ambulance backs up to your door, it won't be practicing, and it is going to cost somebody money—maybe more than you have."

Although this man had to borrow part of the money to pay his first premium, Willson says, "he and the entire family were smiling when I left and expressed their thanks for the time that I had taken to come their way."

Salesmen must sometimes make prospects unhappy, but you do not need to leave them unhappy. A salesman plays a dual role. He is both villain and hero. At first he must be a villain who makes the prospect aware of some need he didn't know he had. But the salesman himself need never pit himslf against the prospect. It is always "me and you against this bug-a-boo," and the salesman exits as the hero who has helped the prospect overcome his problem.

Why a ninety-two-year-old bought life insurance. Joe Rimes, one of our district managers, used the "hot water" technique along with a spectacular word picture to sell a life contract to a 92-year-old man!

"The old gentleman was 92 years of age and announced he definitely would live to be 110. And he probably will, because he did not look to be a day over 60. He was well-to-do, not interested in hospital protection, nor had he ever been interested in insurance of any kind. I looked at him calmly, and, with a smile, said 'Congratulations! It is a pleasure to meet a man like you. From my conversation with you, I observe that you have worked hard to build up an estate, and you have told me that your ambition is to pass it on intact . Have you ever stopped to consider that, at your age, the law of averages may catch up with you before this very day is over? Let's look at the National Mortality Table. You didn't pay your way into this world, but you will surely pay your way out. You don't want to take from your estate, you want to add to it, and insurance is the only way you can prevent loss at death.' That did it. I came away with an annual premium of $100."

Notice how Joe used one standard held by the old fellow: "I don't want to detract from my estate, but pass it on intact," as a lever to get him to adopt another standard—life insurance. Notice how he poured on the hot water: "At your age the law of averages may catch up with you before this very day is over . . . you didn't pay your way into this world, but you are going to have to pay your way out."

Floyd M. Ewton, our regional director in Amarillo had a prospect who offered strong objections to his wife and son wanting accident and health insurance. He wanted to take a chance that nothing would happen to them. Floyd looked out the window and saw a bright shiny new Buick Roadmaster parked in the drive. "Mr. *X*", he said, "Do you have your new Buick insured?"

"Yes," he said, "I certainly do."

"You are a careful driver and don't plan on wrecking the car, do you?"

"No—of course not."

"But at the same time," said Floyd, "you aren't taking any chances on anything happening to that nice new car, are you?"

"Well," Floyd says, "I didn't say anything else—and for a couple of minutes you could have heard a pin drop in that house. Then the husband said in a low voice, 'How much is the annual premium on my wife and boy?' "

J. R. Coarsey, of Madison Real Estate Company, Madison, Tennessee, has developed many subdivisions where thousands of homes now stand. "I always tell them the truth," he says, "and always in a good humor." In telling the truth, he sometimes uses plain talk. "Not long ago," he says, "a man sat down beside me on the bus and said, 'I could have cut your throat the day you sold me a lot by asking my wife if she wasn't ashamed to live with a husband who didn't have enough get-up-and-go to buy a home of his own instead of paying rent. But I now own $3,500 equity in a home, and I could put my arm around you and kiss you for selling me that lot."

Coarsey went right on selling during the depression: "I would draw them a picture of the future and how much more secure it would be if they had a piece of land under them."

One of the big drawbacks to selling real estate, he says, is the firmly ingrained standard that most young people have against "going head-over-heels in debt." "I always impress upon them that buying real estate is an honorable obligation, that it is in a class by itself, and that it is a mark of thriftiness and character to make a commitment to buy a home."

In the chapter on "Desire," we saw that prospects will not act on an idea until you "make it real" to them. "Mr. Jones, have you ever seen a family where the income was cut off for three months? Have you ever seen prized possessions—TV set, home, car—being given up and sold to meet expenses?" An approach like this makes your proposition a lot more "real" than merely saying, "You would need extra money if you were laid off."

C. P. Brown, Sr., a district manager, once called on a man who was habitually behind on his payments. Brown took a tape measure and began to measure the customer. When he asked what the big idea was, Brown said, "Well, it looks like you are going to let your insurance lapse, but my company wants to do something for you anyway—so we are going to send you a nice black shiny casket with your name engraved on it, and we want it to fit you." The customer paid up—and stayed paid up from then on!

Brutal truth closed the sale. L. W. Hildreth, of Cheyenne, Wyoming, spent two and one half hours painting the prospect a picture of an automobile accident involving his wife, his three boys, and himself. He compared the possible cost incurred with an annual premium giving him full protection—hospital and surgery, physicians' service, polio benefits, and accidental death. The prospect still said "no."

Hildreth then pinned the prospect down to a "make-them-say-no" close: "Mr. Prospect," he said, "I am sure from our conversation that Mrs. Prospect feels that some sort of protection such as my company offers is essential to the welfare of her family. Do you feel that it is fair to deprive her of this security?" The prospect sat quietly and said nothing. "Would you like to pay it annually?" asked Hildreth. The prospect said he would and wrote out a check for $198.50.

There is no excuse, ever, for a salesman to be discourteous. There can never be an excuse for the salesman to be disrespectful or insulting. There is no excuse for attempting to use external pressure to force prospects into doing what you want done. But if you are going to be fair to your prospects and to yourself, you must tell them the truth.

The truth is sometimes unpleasant, but if you *are* telling the truth and tell it because you are sincere and feel what you are saying, prospects will not resent it, even if it does make them temporarily uncomfortable. Someone has said that truth is sometimes painful, but that it is antiseptic and leaves no wound. Be that as it may—if you are going to sell at all, you must sometimes have guts enough to tell the truth.

POINTS TO REMEMBER

1. Attempting to apply external pressure—to put pressure on the prospect—is foolish. The very art of salesmanship, however, consists in building up a pressure *inside* the prospect, which can only be relieved when he buys your goods. Desire itself creates an inner pressure, until it is satisfied. And if you are going to arouse desires, you are going to create inner pressure.

2. When a prospect is made to realize that his idea, "I don't want to buy this" is *inconsistent* with some of his other dearly loved ideas, an inner conflict is built up. This inner conflict is resolved only by the prospect changing his mind about "I don't want to buy" or changing the pet idea of his that is in conflict with it.

3. In order to get the prospect to see clearly the inconsistency between his own ideas, you must sometimes tell the hard, plain, unvarnished truth. It is possible to maintain two incompatible, or even contradictory, ideas only if we sugar-coat one of them with "nice words" and make it appear acceptable. Truth is sometimes brutal, but if it is the truth, it never really hurts as much as an untruth would.

18

THE PROSPECT'S OBJECTION
IS YOUR BEST SALES TOOL

A. E. WILLSON, JR., IS CALLING ON A FAMILY
where there are nine children. The older daughter and wife
are being treated for diabetes, and are not insurable. Many insurance salesmen have called on this home, but none have been
able to make a sale.

Willson pins the husband down, and says, "Mr. X, tell me
the real reason you will not buy this insurance."

"Well," said the farmer. "You say you won't write it on my
wife and older daughter. If they can't have it, I don't want
it. Until some salesman tells me he can cover my entire family, there is no use talking to me."

Willson has the real objection out in the open now—and can
figure ways and means of using it to help make the sale. He
turns to the wife.

"Mrs. X," isn't it true that you and your older daughter are
both on diets, and isn't it true that other members of the family
can enjoy many foods that you cannot eat?"

"Yes," she said, "that is certainly true."

"Mrs. X", said Willson, "would you want your entire family
to give up the food that they enjoy—would you want to deny

176

your other children the pleasure of a good meal, merely because you cannot enjoy it?"

"No," she said, "I certainly would not."

"And would you want to deny the other children the benefits of a wonderful hospitalization plan that they are entitled to—because you cannot have it?"

Tears come into the eyes of the farmer's wife. "No, sir, I certainly wouldn't object, and if you will write it on them, it would make me very happy."

Don't Try to Sidestep Objections

Willson has taken an "objection" and turned it into a powerful sales point. Nearly always objections can be used in this manner, if you will take the trouble to find out what the real objection is. Once you know on which peg the entire case against buying hangs, you can nearly always show that this objection is inconsistent with some powerful standard held by the prospect.

To use this power, however, the salesman must get over his fear of the word "No." He must stop avoiding and sidestepping objections and try to bring them to light, where he suspects that they exist. If the prospect has an objection, you aren't going to solve anything by ignoring it. It's there. But you can never deal with it until you know what it is.

W. W. Cordes was once introduced to the vice-president of a firm by the president of the firm. Cordes sensed the prospect wanted the insurance but there was some special reason why he was hesitating, so he asked, "Mr. Blank, tell me the real reason you are hesitating about this."

"Well, to be perfectly frank", said the prospect, "I hate to let the president know that I cannot afford to pay the annual premium."

Cordes assured him that the president would never know, quoted him the quarterly premium, and closed the deal.

A Chinese laundryman once told me very definitely that he would never buy an "accident" policy. I sensed that somehow this prospect objected to the very word "accident." I knew that after he had made a definite commitment that he would not buy an "accident" policy, he would not do so, even if he wanted it, because if he did he would lose face. So, knowing his objection to the word "accident," I spoke of our "health" policy that provided "income" while he might not be able to work. He read over the entire A. & H. policy, liked it and bought it, but as "health insurance" rather than "accident insurance."

John J. Ahearn, Sr., our State Manager in Phoenix, Arizona, sells the prospect in 85 per cent of the leads that he uses. This is an unusual record that John has kept as a "batting average" for many years. His one big secret, he tells me, is using the power in objections. When people don't buy from him, he takes the trouble to find out why. Once he knows the real reason, he goes to work.

John has all his salesmen turn in their lead cards, whether they make a sale or not. He then sends out a different salesman to call on the same prospect. Many times, he says, a prospect will "object" to the salesman himself for no special reason. His personality just doesn't "take" with a particular prospect. So John sends out a different salesman on dead leads, and often finds that the new salesman closes the deal in short order.

A boss' objection to a promotion is overcome. Once you know what the objection is, you can show that this objection is inconsistent with some other strongly held idea—if you know enough about the prospect. You can never know too much about the people you call upon, and never know too much about the product you are selling.

For example, knowing that a certain executive first held a foreman's job at the age of twenty-three would seem to have nothing to do with selling this executive on the idea of making you one of his sales managers. But Gene W. Salter, our District Manager in Hattiesburg, Mississippi, used this knowledge to land his first sales manager's job. Gene was young, and he had nothing to recommend him except his determination and firm conviction that he could handle the job. Conscious of his lack of experience and youthful appearance, he anticipated that the sales executive would probably "object" to putting a mere inexperienced boy in charge of a group of men.

Sure enough, the sales executive did point out these very "reasons" why he couldn't give Gene the job. "It's unfortunate," he said, "but you are just too young to take over such responsibilities."

"Sir," said Gene, "it is my understanding that you were made a foreman in charge of a large group of men when you were just my age. Isn't your present position proof enough that a young man of my age can make good in a supervisory job?"

"For a moment he remained silent, and seemed to be in deep thought," says Gene. "Then he looked up and said, 'You can start Monday.'"

Gene had taken his Sunday punch—his one big "objection" —and used it against him. Turning Gene down for the job could no longer be consistent with the man's ideas about himself. He *had* to give Gene the job or else admit his inconsistency.

Objections Can Increase Your Sales Power

There is another way that objections and no's can be turned to good account. Any salesman who has ever tried the experiment knows that the more difficult the sale, the more sales power he seems able to tap—the more his determination is to win out over the "no" rather than to accept it as defeat.

You often hear a salesman say, in some surprise, "It seemed hopeless—but I made up my mind I was going to sell him and something happened to me. I sold as I had never sold before."

For example, I have heard Russ C. Rosson, our Regional Director, tell how he called on a large appliance dealer and asked for an appointment.

"I was seated in the waiting room and waited as patiently as possible for about an hour. The dealer, himself, finally came out and explained that he was on his way to lunch, and since he had noted from my card that I was in the insurance business, he did not feel that he could give me any time, as he was well covered by personal insurance, and besides he did all this type of business with an old friend.

"Well, it seemed like a good enough objection, and I was about to give it up, when I remembered something you said to me when I first came to work with you about the bigger the challenge, the more power would come to your aid—*if* you determined to deal with the challenge rather than run away from it. I decided that this was a good test case, and made up my mind to accept these "no's" as challenges.

"I explained to this gentleman that I would like to go along and have lunch with him (suddenly I seemed to have more self-confidence and boldness), since my proposition was so unusual and would afford him such a wonderful opportunity that I felt it would be worth his time. He reluctantly gave me the interview, and I found myself selling as I had never sold before. I seemed to have just the right word at the right time, and I enjoyed every minute of it. The result was that I sold him the Resident Director Plan and later became a personal friend. He confided to me that he had been using that very objection on insurance men for years."

"Must" means "can." A river that meets no obstructions has little power. Place a dam across it, and the backed-up water becomes a powerful force. Psychologists tell us that our emotions work the same way. As long as everything is going smoothly and you are meeting no resistance, you have little or no emotional power. You don't need any. Emotion comes into being only when some outlet of expression is blocked, or appears blocked—or when some difficulty needs to be faced. Then, you find yourself with a power that you cannot call up by mere will power.

When you face the challenge, the power comes of its own accord. When a man is chased by a bull, the five-foot fence that seems to shut him off from safety adds strength to his legs that they never possessed before—if his main thought is to get over it. Several years ago, the newspapers carried an account of a housewife who fought her way out of her basement and routed an escaped circus lion that blocked the stair.

The "no's" and objections that the prospect puts up in front of you as obstacles can automatically increase your sales power —if you take them as challenges instead of discouragements.

J. M. Mathis, tells how he called on a prospect in San Angelo, who locked the screen door in his face and announced that he did not believe in insurance and that no insurance agent would get through that door. "For some reason," says Mathis, "I decided I was going to sell him—right through that screen door. I asked if I might just explain my plan—and he said 'No.' I then asked whether he would like me to save him $500 to $1,000. He said, 'Anyone likes to save money.' I don't remember everything I said, but I do remember that I did the best selling job through that screen door that I had ever done—and I remember getting the feeling that I could sell anybody as long as that feeling lasted. At the end of my pitch, he opened the door and said, "I've never had it explained to me that way before. Just write me that plan on the annual basis."

How to Handle Third-Party Objectors

Have you ever been right in the middle of your pitch, and had some relative, friend or "advisor" of the prospect come in and interrupt with comments or objections? Sometimes, two or three words are all that are necessary to completely kill a sale.

A. L. Flora, our regional director in Richmond, Va., has the answer for turning these objectors into allies. "Third-party interference — relatives and friends who popped in at the wrong time and offered advice — used to get me down," he says. "Then one day I got to thinking: What makes these people so anxious to give advice? Why does anyone want to give advice? The answer, it seems to me, is *ego*. These people want to get into the act. They want to feel important. Once I figured out that ego was what motivated these people, I discovered I could use that same ego to help me make the sale. Since they were anxious to get into the act, I made them the star performer. I began to direct my remarks to these third parties.

Since they were anxious to give advice, I even began to ask for their advice myself: 'Mr. Blank, don't you agree that . . .'; 'Mrs. X, what do you think about this? We are trying to decide which type of policy would be best for Mr. Jones. Now here are the facts, and I would like you to help us make a decision.' This gets the third party on your side and in your corner, for he realizes that he can continue to star in your presentation only so long as he plays your game.

I also try to get the third party to voice any objections he may have while I am there, otherwise he can tear my sales pitch to shreds after I leave my prospect. I now welcome these intruders, for they have helped me make many a sale."

A nagging wife helps a sale. Many times a wife or husband can play the role of silent objectors. I remember one case where I directed all my sales pitch to the husband, and had him on the verge of signing up. The wife stayed back in the kitchen, but would dash out at the most inopportune moment and shout — "I'd think about that a while," or, "Why do you think you need more insurance?" or, "Where are you going to get the money to buy any more insurance?"

Finally, I stepped down the hall and called to her, "Mrs. Blank, if you can spare the time, I wish you would help us out a little here. We are talking about something that vitally concerns you — in fact, it concerns you more than anyone else, and we would like to know what you think about it." She dried her hands and came into the living room.

"Did you hear all the various points to this plan as I explained them to Mr. Blank?" I asked.

"No," she said, "but I think I got the gist of it."

"Well," I said, "it is important enough to you for me to want you to know all about it — so I will go over it again briefly, just for you."

She turned out not to be a bad-tempered woman at all. Her ego was somewhat hurt because we had not consulted her before. "Mr. Blank never discusses his business with me," she said.

"Well," I replied, "this is one thing that is your business — and Mr. Blank and I want to discuss it with you." She made the sale for me.

The same psychology applies to lawyers and bankers who are called in by the prospect as consultants. Once the prospect calls in a professional advisor, direct all your remarks to the advisor. Let him know that you respect his opinion. Whether or not he knows anything about the product you're selling, give him credit for being an expert on the subject. In this way you sell the "advisor" to the prospect. Human nature being what it is, the "advisor" will then turn around and sell you to the prospect.

Without this strategy for handling third parties, the salesman can very easily lose command of the selling situation.

And like a football team which has lost the ball, the salesman who has lost command of the situation isn't going to score any points.

"No" Need Not Be Final

Remember that "No" is not final until the salesman accepts it in his own mind as such. Bruce Barton tells of a cash register salesman who tried for ten years to sell Marshall Field, of Chicago. Finally, on the tenth try, he got an order for $150,000. "Well," he said, "$15,000 per year isn't so bad."

Some time ago *Your Life* magazine ran a short statement by John M. Wilson, vice-president of The National Cash Register Company, on the difference between "disappointment" and "discouragement" upon hearing "No." It is so fitting that I want to quote it here:

"Recently, I congratulated a salesman upon securing a fine order," said Wilson. "The salesman had been trying for years to obtain some business from this particular company, but without results. He agreed he had met many disappointments at their hands, but he smiled and said, 'I always remember that they can say *no* a thousand times, but it takes only one *yes* for me to get the order.' He is one who thoroughly understands the difference between disappointment and discouragement. Though we are all going to experience many disappointments, we must never permit ourselves to be overcome by discouragement. We have no control over the disappointments we are certain to meet, but it is by our own decision that we become discouraged. . . .

"Discouragement means exactly what it says: Loss of courage, disintegration of the spirit — failure. A disappointment is a natural reaction, but when a man yields to discouragement, the fight is over. He has given up. . . . Disappointment can be a *spur to improvement* that will contribute to success. But discouragement is a mortal enemy that destroys courage and robs one of the will to fight. . . . It is not circumstance that causes disappointment, but one's own reaction to that circumstance.

"Everyone must meet disappointment, many times; it is simply a part of life. When it is met, we may resign ourselves to discouragement and failure. Or we may recognize *each disappointment as an asset by which we can profit*, and take *new strength* from a lesson learned."

"*Across the river and into the trees.*" A few years ago, I was bird-hunting down in East Texas with a friend. We had an old farmer along with us who knew where the coveys were to be found. Our dog flushed a covey and we took a shot. The covey flew across the creek. We waded across and took another shot and the covey flew right back across the creek. We waded back again, took a shot, and the birds flew back across to the other side. This happened three times. I then asked the old farmer, "How many more times are we going to have to cross this creek?" He replied, "Every time we get to it." A salesman should be prepared to wrestle with an objection, every time he gets to it."

POINTS TO REMEMBER

1. Objections can be your most valuable sales tool. You can use them to make the sale, if you know what they are. You can't use them, however, if you don't know what they are. So, don't be afraid of objections. Don't be afraid they will come out. And if they don't come out, *dig* them out.

2. A small stream may display no power as long as it meets no obstacles or objections. Place a dam across it, however, and that small stream will build up a tremendous power that may generate millions of kilowatts of electricity. Obstacles also dam up the power in a man. Objections actually cause you automatically to draw upon your inner powers, and imbue you with much more sales power—if you regard them as challenges and make up your mind you are going to overcome them.

3. "Third-party" objectors can either make or break the sale, depending upon how you handle them. Resent them, fight them, attempt to show them up or discredit them, and they will break your sale, either while you're present or by talking you down after you leave. Listen to them, talk to them, build them up in the eyes of the prospect, and they will very often step in and make the sale for you.

19

IF YOU WANT TO BE
A STAR SALESMAN,
PUT ON A SHOW

THOMAS EDISON WAS ONE INVENTOR WHO DID not die poor. The reason was that Edison, in addition to being a good inventor, was also a master salesman. Shortly after he invented the incandescent light, for example, Edison hit upon an idea to publicize his new invention and "make it real" to the people. He would light up one square mile of New York City!

To get permission to do this, Edison invited aldermen from New York to his laboratory. He took them into a dimly-lit room, where a single lamp was the only source of light. When they were all gathered together in the semi-dark room, Edison called out "Turn up the lights," and an assistant threw a switch that flooded the room with light from many electric lights. There, before the astonished aldermen, was a table set for a feast — complete with a bottle of champagne at each place.

Edison could have spent hours trying to tell these men about the electric light — how much better it was than old fashioned lamps, how nice it would be to have a square mile

185

of the city lit up. Instead, he put on a show for them and let them see for themselves. His unusual and dramatic presentation got him permission for his pet project in short order.

Today the word *spectacular* is used to describe one of those million-dollar television shows that is so unusual, so star-studded, that the audience is almost forced to look, out of curiosity if nothing else. The word *spectacular* literally means something so unusual or arresting that you are forced to look at it. From the same root word we get inspect (to look into closely), *spectator* (one who looks on), and so on. Long before television was invented, power salesmen were putting on "spectaculars," to cause prospects to "stop — *look* — and remain to listen." The "spectacular" can be used in connection with each of the five points of making the sale. You can be spectacular in your approach, in arousing desire, and in closing.

Christian P. Sorensen, a contractor in Baltimore, was having little success in getting bricklayers until he thought up a "spectacular" newspaper ad. Sorensen was building a 600-unit apartment house, and he needed bricklayers desperately. First he tried all the usual orthodox methods of getting bricklayers interested in working for him. He went to the labor union, the employment agencies, and ran the usual run of classified ad: "Bricklayers wanted."

When Sorensen was about ready to give up, he hit upon an idea. By adding just one word to his newspaper ad — he soon had more bricklayers than he knew what to do with.

He ran a new ad that read: WANTED: *Left-handed* Bricklayers."

The ad didn't tell *why* he wanted left-handed bricklayers. But the next morning his office was overrun by bricklayers who were curious to find out. Most of the bricklayers who applied — and were hired — turned out to be right-handed bricklayers, who only pretended to be left-handed in order to find out about the ad. They never did find out — for Sorensen himself didn't know why he wanted left-handed bricklayers — but the ad got him more bricklayers than he could use.

What Makes People "Look"?

We look at the unusual and the unexpected. We look at that which is different. We only casually glance at the "same old scenery" and listen half-way, if at all, to the "same old story." But let something new and different appear on the scene, and right away we are all eyes and all ears. Motion also attracts the eye. Perhaps this goes back to our primitive past, when our ancestors had to be wary of any moving object they sighted in the woods. A still object offered little threat. But motion could mean danger. Whatever the reason, our eyes are automatically attracted to an object in motion, in preference to an object at rest. This is the reason that advertising firms now use "animated" billboards.

Back in 1947, Mr. T. H. Parham and I had a subdivision out from Dallas that was located several hundred feet off the main highway. For some reason we just couldn't get people to drive over and look at our lots. We put up signs along the highway, but ordinary signs seemed to attract little or no attention. Then we hit upon the idea of buying up some war-surplus balloons. We purchased a dozen of these large balloons, filled them with gas, and painted on them: "Lot Sale — Special Low Prices." We then raised these balloons over the property to a height of about 200 feet. They attracted so much attention that we soon had more prospects than we had bargained for, and had a traffic problem on our hands. We did sell out the subdivision, however, in short order.

All Prospects Are from Missouri

It isn't only people from Missouri who must be "shown" to believe. All of us are much more impressed after we see something with our own eyes.

In 1852, Elisha Otis worked in a bedspread factory. In order to speed up construction, he built an elevator in the factory, and in the process invented something new — a safety brake that would prevent the elevator from falling if the cable broke. Otis started trying to sell his invention, but nobody was interested. He told them about it, and elevator manufacturers said they believed him — but they were not moved to buy.

The next year Otis went to the Crystal Palace Exhibition in Bryant Park, New York. He built a tall scaffolding on the mid-way and constructed an elevator. Several times a day Otis would have himself lifted in the elevator to the very top of the scaffolding. Then, while he hung there, an assistant would cut the rope. As spectators watched, spellbound, the elevator would remain where it was, and Otis would call down calmly, "Perfectly safe, ladies and gentlemen, perfectly safe."

This spectacular stunt caused such a demand for Otis' elevators that he was forced to go into the business of producing them himself.

Personal friends can sometimes be the most difficult to sell. In the early days of our company, I tried unsuccessfully several times to interest a friend of mine in a $10,000 mortgage-protection policy. He did not have sufficient funds to meet many of the necessities that would arise in the event of his death, and I felt his wife needed this protection. He still owed around $10,000 on his home, as well as many other bills, but somehow he wasn't interested in mortgage protection.

In order to bring these possibilities home to him in a realistic manner, I went back to the office and had a check prepared in the amount of $10,000, payable to his wife "after the claim blanks in the recent death of her husband, John L. Smith, had been approved." This check was mailed to Mrs. Smith. The next day I got a call from him, and although he attempted to pass it off as a joke, I knew from his tone of voice that he was somewhat concerned and that it had really shaken him up a little bit. He said, "I'm still not interested in buying any insurance, but when you come by this way next time I would like to find out about what this policy would pay, and what it would cost me." I called back by and wrote a contract for $10,000 mortgage protection, and eventually sold him, in addition, $40,000 straight life protection.

Tom High, at the time our manager in Atlanta, Georgia, had tried unsuccessfully three times to interest a druggist in hospitalization insurance. The prospect "couldn't see it."

Then one day Tom went by to have a cup of coffee at the
drug store and approached the subject of hospitalization once
more. The prospect still "couldn't see it." As Tom pulled
his wallet from his pocket to pay for his coffee, he accidentally
dropped three claim checks on the floor. The checks were all
in large amounts — the smallest being for several hundred
dollars.

The druggist got down to help Tom pick up the checks.
"What are these?" he asked.

"Oh," said Tom, "those are just a few claim checks I am on
the way to deliver in person" as if it were a routine matter.

The druggist immediately became curious, and wanted to
know what the claims were for. Tom then explained the
calamity that had befallen each claimant. Nothing more was
said about selling insurance. But as Tom started to go the
druggist said, "Mr. High, if you have time this afternoon
around five o'clock you might stop in, and I'll talk to you
about that hospitalization protection for me and my family."

Having seen with his own eyes actual claim checks, at last
he could "see" hospitalization insurance.

Seeing is believing. Salesmen should always remember that
there is a tremendous difference between *hearing* and *seeing*
and between *knowing* and *seeing.* You can see this in everyday
life — in many fields other than salesmanship. For example,
a city will go along with lax fire protection. Every thinking
man in town "knows" that it is possible for a hotel to catch
fire and kill hundreds of citizens. But no one does anything
about it.

Then, there *is* a disastrous hotel fire. Now that it has happened, everyone "knows" it in a different way. Editorials appear in the newspapers. Citizens groups are founded. In-
vestigating committees are appointed. The fire department
is reorganized. But, in two or three years, they will have
forgotten that buildings can catch fire, and will fall back into
the same old rut again, unless some public-spirited civic
salesman can keep before them the picture of what can happen,
in a real and dramatic fashion.

One of the brochures we mail out is entitled, "You have

heard — but have you *seen* what disability can do?" The brochure is a dramatic word picture of a family having its TV set and furniture moved out, losing their automobile, and, at last, losing their home, because of disability.

Remington-Rand salesmen go out and take pictures of disastrous fires where important files have been destroyed. Then when they call on a prospect for one of Remington-Rand's fireproof filing cabinets, they show the prospect these pictures.

"Mr. Jones, here is a picture of a fire that happened on (date). There was a loss of $30,000. Look at these ordinary file cabinets here that were burned and their entire contents destroyed. Documents were lost that can never be recovered."

Now, the prospect *knows* all along that these things can happen. He knows that his own file cabinets are not fireproof, but this bit of "showmanship" makes him know it in a different way.

In our various businesses we use the Polaroid Land Camera quite a bit to take pictures that can later be used as showmanship in selling. The Polaroid Land Camera salesmen themselves use this technique of "show them" as well as tell them. Most people today have heard or read about the Polaroid camera which takes a picture and develops it on the spot. They know the camera will do this. But when a Polaroid salesman puts a camera in the hands of a prospect, shows him how to operate it, lets him take a picture, and, 60 seconds later, pulls the picture from the back of the camera, the prospect is always more or less surprised and thrilled. "Well — what do you know? What about that? It really works, doesn't it?" is a common reaction.

How to Become a "Star" Salesman

To be a "star" you must first become an "actor."

Jerry Gelpi, our Regional Manager in Jackson, Miss., wrote to me as follows, when I asked for some comment from him to include in this book:

"In selling you must be an actor. You must in many ways act according to the whims of the purchaser. If you would be a topnotch salesman, and by this of course we mean one who closes the greatest percentage of sales per calls, you must be adaptable enough to cope with each new problem or problems made manifest by the fact that each prospect is a new and different personality."

Jerry goes on to say that when he talks to the prospect, he "acts out" his talk. If he is picturing to the prospect the possibility of an automobile accident, and the need to provide against such possibilities, he may say something like:

"Mr. Jones, you may be the most careful driver in the world. But suppose some day you meet a drunk on the highway, who is weaving down the road at 70 or 80 miles on hour (illustrated by making a weaving motion of the hand). You look for a place to turn out of the way (Jerry looks back and forth), but there is none. (Jerry then becomes an imaginary driver of an automobile. He wrestles with the steering wheel. He puts on brakes.) But there is nothing you can do — and this drunk crashes into your car (smashes fist into open palm).

A play is no more real than a book. But it seems more real when it is "acted out."

I have seen Floyd Ewton reach over and "chop off" a prospect's leg with the heel of his hand as he explained the protection afforded in case of loss of limb. You can use drama in many little ways in your sales presentation. Just remember that, in order to be dramatic, a presentation must have *movement* if it is to be life-like. Things that are alive move. Imagine the best actors and actresses in the world sitting on a stage reading the lines of a play from their chairs. There is no reality to it. The whole thing is dead and uninteresting. But when they add the ingredient of "action" to the very same lines, the play becomes so life-like you almost forget that it isn't really happening.

A fountain pen can be a magic wand. P. L. Bordelon, our branch manager in Tupelo, Mississippi, uses his fountain pen to achieve drama. He takes his pen from his pocket when he first begins his pitch. He then uses it to make gestures, to draw diagrams, to make pictures. He hands the pen to the prospect and "gets him into the act" by asking him to figure with it. In his hands, an ordinary fountain pen almost becomes a magic wand that brings his words to life.

"Keep doing something all through the presentation," he says. "This keeps the interest of the prospect alive, for he is waiting to see what you will do next. One of the best things to do is to begin filling out the application blank from the very beginning of your presentation."

People have a certain amount of curiosity about any action — and about anything that is in the least bit different. Witness the sidewalk superintendents who gather around and watch a power shovel at work in a downtown excavation. There is nothing exciting, or thrilling, or suspenseful, about a shovel lifting dirt out of the ground and depositing it on a truck, over and over again. But the shovel *is* in motion — and it *is* doing something *different*.

They Danced into the Bank!

I am a director of the Merchant State Bank in Dallas. Some time ago, the president of the bank, Mr. William Beavers, suggested that the bank have square dances from time to time on the parking lot adjoining the bank. There was some opposition to the idea, for some of the directors felt that square dances weren't quite the thing for a dignified institution like a bank to get mixed up in. We voted, however, to have the dances.

The idea behind the dances was to get to know our customers better, show our appreciation for their business — and perhaps creates a "friendly" feeling for the bank. Square dances are not at all unusual in Texas. In fact, they are so common that they are almost a part of the scenery. It seems, however, that when a *bank* gives a square dance, it is spectacular.

Our dances created quite a stir, and many people probably came out of curiosity to see what sort of a dance a bank would throw for the public. New faces began to appear in the bank. Many people dropped around to tell Mr. Beavers what a good time they had the Saturday night before — and remained to open an account.

So remember, you don't have to be very *different* to attract attention.

POINTS TO REMEMBER

1. People look at the unusual, the different, the unexpected. Capitalize on this.

2. People look at objects in motion, in preference to objects at rest.

3. Don't just *tell* them, but *show* them that it has happened and can happen to you.

4. To become a star salesman, become an actor. Put on a show. Act out your sales pitch.

5. Make your presentation as life-like as possible.

20

WHEN THE SCIENCE OF SALESMANSHIP BECOMES AN ART

USED TO READ EVERY BOOK ON SALESMANSHIP I could get my hands on, and frequently attended lectures and courses. But somehow, none of them ever seemed to improve my salesmanship very much. Much of this was really excellent advice. One reason it didn't help me any more than it did was simply that I did not put it into practice. I would read the book and say to myself, "Well, I'll try to remember that, and see if my sales improve."

"Remembering" good advice never helps anyone, however. You must practice it until it becomes habitual.

Another reason books on salesmanship never helped me any more than they did was that I would read a chapter where the author said, "Do this," or, "Say this to the prospect." I would then go out and go through the motions of doing what he recommended in a mechanical way — and if I tried his recommended sentences at all — I parroted them in a mechanical way.

The prospect is not a mechanical robot that you can feed a "sales sentence" into at the top and have a "sale" drop out the bottom, like a piece of gum, after you have inserted a coin in the machine. Prospects are people. And because of this, salesmanship is both a science and an art. Salesmen speak of the "game" of salesmanship, the "romance" of salesmanship. You need an "extra something" to turn a science into an art, a game, or a romance.

I was talking to Dr. George Reeves, President, Chapman College, California, and he said, "Pierce, I call this 'extra something' *selling with your heart*. You can learn technique of salesmanship and never make a salesman," he says, "unless you learn to get your heart and soul into your work — and apply what you learn with your heart as well as your head. Enthusiasm, faith, spirit, a strong feeling for other people — these are all things of the heart. The good salesman has a *feeling* for salesmanship as well as a knowledge about it."

"We produce in others the attitudes and feelings we show in ourselves," says Karl S. Bernhardt, Ph.D., Professor of Psychology, University of Toronto, in his book *Practical Psychology*.* "For instance, if we are trying to interest someone in something, it is necessary to show intense interest ourselves, for interest tends to be infectious. A frank, cheerful manner tends to produce the same in return. So, in order to produce in others a desirable set of attitudes, the first essential is for the individual to show these attitudes himself."

B. T. Gargus, Manager of our Special Life Division, had this advice recently in his newsletter to salesmen:

"A negative question calls for a negative answer. By the same token, a negative attitude brings a negative response. But, confidence breeds confidence. Think positive."

H. W. Chrisman, Manager of our Winchester, Virginia, office, practices what he calls "Helping the prospect say 'yes.'" He does this by maintaining a "yes" attitude of mind himself. If you have an affirmative attitude, he says, you will produce an affirmative attitude in the prospect.

Why Gloomy Gus Can't Sell

Have you ever noticed that on those days when you get up on the wrong side of the bed and are "soured on the world,"

---

* N. Y.: McGraw-Hill Book Co., Inc., 1953.

you invariably have a bad sales day? You may sell as hard as ever — use the same techniques as any other day — but your temporary deprecatory attitude toward the world and the people in it detract from your power to get close to people, to move them and influence them. The quality that human beings are most sensitive to is your estimation of their worth. And prospects will reflect your own attitude back towards you.

Larry Breeden, sales director of one of our companies in Corpus Christi, Texas, says that he has learned when he gets up in the morning with a grouch against the world either not to try to sell at all, or else get over the grouch.

He says that if you can have a good laugh with the prospect, it makes you more human, and gets you closer to the prospect: "I have found that if you once get people to laugh with you, it is much easier to instill confidence in them. The American public like a regular Joe Doakes to sell them. They don't like a pretty boy or a fast talker. They want just a plain, down-to-earth regular guy."

Optimism Is Magic

Once we understand that *our own attitudes* have an influence on the other person — and have a strong tendency to induce a similar attitude *in him*, it is easy to understand why the optimistic salesman can outsell his pessimistic brother.

C. M. Dennis, one of our managers, calls it "keeping the prospect happy." If you are pessimistic about your own job — about the future — and about the world in general, says Dennis, this attitude gets over to the prospect and causes him to feel pessimistic. Optimism is an expensive, generous emotion, while pessimism is a restrictive, miserly emotion. Why should the prospect buy your product when he feels so pessimistic about the future? Optimism not only loosens the muscles and makes the prospect feel better, it opens his purse strings as well.

Joseph A. Kennedy, in his booklet, "Relax and Sell," tells how numerous experiments have proved beyond a doubt that a person is more generous, more liberal with his money, more in a "spending mood," when is is feeling optimistic, than when he is feeling pessimistic.

C. M. Dennis keeps his own salesmen happy (and productive) by a fine human relations program that doesn't allow gripes and complaints to become chronic. "If you have a gripe or complaint, don't be timid about telling me about it," he says. "I am interested in you — and I want to help you with any problems. As long as you make them known, we can cure them together, and both stay in a good humor."

This policy has paid many dividends to Dennis, for his good-humored salesmen bring in the apps.

Learn to Appreciate People

Insurance Index has called National Banker's Life Insurance Company the fastest growing insurance company in the U. S. In nine years time, Nablico has come up from a business with $25,000 in assets to $10,000,000 and it's still growing. This growth is possible only because our managers, agents and salesmen work *for* the company — in more ways than one. Our motto from the beginning has been "We appreciate our agents." Because we do appreciate them, they work with us and for us, to a degree that amazes many outsiders. This motto was not chosen idly.

If you look up the word *appreciate* in the dictionary you will find that it comes from the Latin *ad,* meaning *to,* and *pretium,* meaning *price.* The definition my dictionary gives is: "To appraise, estimate, or value; also to value justly, esteem highly; recognize the worth or quality of; to raise in value (opposed to depreciate)."

We believe we have the best salesmen in the world — we "esteem them highly" — and they in turn, make this belief true by their production records.

What is your estimation of the people you call upon? How do you value them in your own mind? Do you regard them as "my bread and butter," as victims to be exploited, as "the masses" — or do you respect them for the unique, individual personality that each person is?

All this has a bearing on how well you are able to apply the science of salesmanship and turn it into an art. Prospects will not warm up to a salesman who does not appreciate them. Have you ever noticed that the best salesmen are always good natured fellows, who laugh a lot and get a big kick out of being with people? Good salesmen like people. They like them with all their faults and shortcomings. They like people in spite of cussedness and peculiarities. And because they do have a deep liking for people *as people*, people like them.

The Golden Rule Is Still Golden

Henry Ford once said, "I am convinced by my own experience and by that of others, that if there is any one secret of success it lies in the ability to get the other person's point of view and see things from his angle as well as your own."

Owen D. Young said, "The man who can put himself in the place of other men, who can understand the workings of their minds, need never worry about what the future has in store for him."

A friend of mine, Ben Jack Cage, has been successful as an insurance executive, a boat manufacturer, and also in the manufacture of air conditioners for automobiles. Not long ago I asked him how it was possible for a man to be successful in such apparently unrelated businesses, and at the same time. We usually think that for a man to become successful in a certain business, he must devote so much time to learning the ropes of that particular business, he has little time to get to be an expert in any other business.

"Well, Pierce," he said, "whether you're building boats, running an insurance business, or manufacturing air conditioners, there is one common demoninator in all businesses. In each of these businesses you are dealing with *people*, and that's the really important thing. Learn how to deal with people and you have acquired valuable experience for any type of business."

John Ben Shepperd, Attorney General for the State of Texas, has told me, "Understanding people is more important for a lawyer than understanding law."

In this book I have tried to tell you some of the "laws" or "rules" of the science of salesmanship. But, just as John Ben Shepperd says that understanding people is more important than understanding law — so is understanding people more important to the salesman, than understanding the "rules." That's what turns the science of salesmanship into an art.

When I began writing this book, I went to my old friend John Bennick, President of Oil Industries Life, Houston, Texas, and asked him to give me his one big "sales secret" to include in the book. This is what he wrote me:

Perhaps the greatest sales thought which I have used and one which has been of immeasurable value to me in dealing with any and all types of people — one which has certainly been a strong factor in closing a large volume of business — is the ability to constantly place and keep myself and my thinking in the position of my prospect. It has given me a much better understanding of what I would do if I were in the prospect's place, what I would desire as to the type of business or contract I would want, how I would want to pay, how much I could afford, and many other factors which, if presented to the prospect as I would desire them and could handle them, makes easier decisions and a much larger percentage of sales per interview.

Needless to say, this same philosophy applies in getting a larger percentage of interviews. It is my feeling that notwithstanding the tremendous value of a razor-sharp presentation, well polished prospecting and interview-making methods and dynamic closes, none of them is of sufficient value to place them ahead of the ability to "keep one's self in the position of the prospect."

A. R. Craig, manager of our Agency Department, recently sent out the following in his "flash" bulletin to our salesmen:

"Try this plan for one week: Before you see the prospect, think long and seriously of what you have to offer him. Consider it from his point of view. See what the advantage would be to *you*, if *you* were this prospect, to buy. *Be him* before you see him. On the strength of the points you are to present, *would you buy?*"

In writing this book, I have tried to tell you the *principles* that I have used, and that hundreds of others in our organizations have used, to bring success in selling. The story is all there. And the same principles can work as well for you as they have for me and many others. But whether they will or not is now largely up to you. A book in itself is a cold and lifeless thing. Only if you let it arouse *your* enthusiasm, *your* will to sell, *your* faith and confidence, can its message come alive for you. Try to apply these methods mechanically, and they will have no power for you. Memorizing my own sales sentences word-for-word will not close any sales for you. For you, too, are not a vending machine. You can't insert this book in a slot at the top and have a sales success come out. Instead, read and digest the book — and let it become a part of *you*. Then its message will come out in *your* words, and its methods will work through *your* ways. Then you'll find you are a Power Salesman in your own right, and in your own way.

POINTS TO REMEMBER

1. Prospects are people, not machines.

2. Because they are people, your own attitudes are equally as important as your techniques and your knowledge.

3. In order to work with people effectively, you must put yourself in the other fellow's place and "Do unto others as you would have them do unto you", if you were the other person.

4. When you try to use another person's techniques without making them your own, you use them mechanically, and ineffectively. Digest the principles of power in this book, practice them and work on them until they become *yours*—and you'll be a power salesman.

5. Keep plugging.

This book ends here.

Your Power Selling begins here!